Issues in Faith and History

Papers presented at the second Edinburgh conference on
Dogmatics, 1987

edited by
Nigel M. de S. Cameron

RUTHERFORD HOUSE BOOKS
Edinburgh

Published by Rutherford House, 17 Claremont Park,
Edinburgh EH6 7PJ, Scotland

SCOTTISH BULLETIN OF EVANGELICAL THEOLOGY
SPECIAL STUDY 3

ISBN 0 946068 37 2

Computer typeset at Rutherford House on Apple Macintosh™
Printed in Great Britain by BPCC Wheatons Ltd, Exeter

Contents

Issues in Faith and History
Edited by Nigel M. de S. Cameron
Papers read at the Third Edinburgh Conference in Christian
Dogmatics, 1987

Preface

At the heart of the intellectual crisis of the modern church lies
the cluster of questions which centre on the relations of
history and faith. Most obviously, there arises the problematic
of Holy Scripture. How accessible should we expect the
'Word of God written' to be to scrutiny according to the
contemporary canons of historiography? To put it otherwise,
what parameters are appropriate to the definition of an
historical method which will be able to interpret Scripture –
without, *ex hypothesi* systematically erasing the supernatural
from its record; both in detail and, indeed, in the scope and
character of the whole? How may the canonical character of
Scripture properly determine the church's *hermeneutica sacra?*

Much of the past century's theological attention has been
focused on the interpretation of the Bible. Yet the issues of
faith and history go well beyond even that wide area of
concern. The range of the papers which follow both
demonstrate this, and establish something else: that
conservative, Protestant orthodoxy has more than caught up
with discussions from which it was once by choice excluded.
No longer can it be said that conservative evangelical theology
is possible only for those who live before the rise of critical
history, with all its momentous implications for our
understanding of the past and, supremely, of this religion
which defines itself by revelation in history. The energetic
scholarship and intellectual candour of the essays which
follow reveal something of the tone of contemporary
conservative theology, and enshrine a continuing challenge to
the still-dominant consensus which seeks, defiantly, to remain
at odds with the tradition. As they range from contemporary
Continental theology to the theology of Africa, from biblical
interpretation to ethics, the mapping of areas of current
theological concern goes hand in hand with confidence in the
authenticity of the historic faith.

1

These papers were first delivered at the Second Edinburgh Conference in Christian Dogmatics, convened at Rutherford House in August of 1987. This biennial conference brings together theologians from Britain and overseas in a common concern for the engagement of the church in a theological enterprise which is both faithful to its past, and open to its future, and the breaking forth of yet more light from God's most holy Word.

Nigel M. de S. Cameron
Rutherford House, Edinburgh
January 23rd, 1989

ON GIVING HOPE IN A SUFFERING WORLD: RESPONSE TO MOLTMANN

Stephen N. Williams

Theology and history – the marriage is looking pretty firm these days and few would wish to rend asunder what a generation of theologians have joined together. Most vigorous amongst Western European promoters of this alliance in the heady sixties were Pannenberg and Moltmann. Pannenberg is treated elsewhere in this collection[1] and it would be unfittingly discriminating to eschew some consideration of Moltmann. It is intrinsically his due on account of the fact that he has kept up both the quality and the course of the theological work which attained publicity with *Theology of Hope* in the sixties.[2] His latest major work, *God in Creation*, provokes discussion that is still largely within the orbit of 'theology and history' and general discussion of his work will presumably receive stimulus from the very recent publication of the first comprehensive treatment of Moltmann's thought up to 1979.[3] I select for investigation here 'hope and suffering'; limit it to a few questions; focus on issues that arise, not on exposition of Moltmann's thought. The question of theodicy is not only intrinsically important, it has to do in contemporary theology with the relation of historical experience to the eschatological end of history, *inter alia*. This is certainly the case with Moltmann. So the theme is fitting for us.

A recent article by Richard Bauckham on Theodicy from Ivan Karamazov to Moltmann will launch our discussion nicely.[4] Bauckham argues that an adequate theological theodicy in the contemporary context requires two things. First, it must avoid any proposal that makes suffering *necessary* to God's purposes or, indeed, to any purposes of human origin. Such necessity would collide with the justified

1. T. Bradshaw, God's Relationship to History in Pannenberg.
2. London, 1967.
3. R. Bauckham, *Moltmann: Messianic Theology in the Making*, Basingstoke, 1987. *God in Creation*, appeared in 1985.
4. *Modern Theology*, 4.1, 1987, pp. 83-97.

3

sense of moral outrage at suffering. Secondly, it 'must contain an initiative for overcoming suffering'[5] and proceed to embody a counter-movement to combat suffering. Strictly, Bauckham claims that this is *de facto* what modernity requires in theodicy - not that the requirements are justified *tout court* but he clearly sympathizes with them and, more to our present point, Moltmann takes on board such proposals.

How does Moltmann respond? In the first phase of his work, by holding forth Christian eschatological hope. This is not to justify suffering but it promises that suffering will be overcome. By setting divine promise in contradiction to present worldly reality, it created in those who hope an energy to fight what is eschatologically doomed and to establish at least anticipations of what is eschatologically destined – cosmic righteousness. We have, then, a mobilizing eschatological theodicy. In the second phase (represented by the second major work, *The Crucified God*) the claim is made that God is himself identified with the suffering in suffering and he takes up the suffering of humanity into his own. This is what the cross tells a suffering world. In this incarnational identification with Jesus, God does not just assist the liberation of the suffering by comfort but by siding with them he protests against the suffering of the world and thus will not remain at rest in it. He is 'the protesting God'.[6] That is it in outline, though Bauckham sets forth in some detail the force of the modern requirement for theodicy and Moltmann's response.

A difficulty with an otherwise helpful account is that the nature of necessity is unclear. Bauckham makes much of those theodicies that must be rejected that make suffering *necessary* to the fulfilment of the divine purposes. He includes under this heading the famous freewill defence sponsored most prominently today by Alvin Plantinga to whose work he does not (and probably need not) refer. A key proposition in the freewill defence is that freedom to actualize a possibility, the possibility of moral evil, is constitutive of human being; strictly, what is often argued is that this enables (along with some other proposition, perhaps relating to

5. *Ibid.*, p. 89.
6. *The Crucified God,* London, 1974, p. 226.

4

natural evil) *logically* some defence of theism – whether it is *theologically* warranted is a matter of theology, not of logical coherence.[7] Now any *necessity* of suffering to the divine purpose take on a different guise in the context of *freedom* and *possibility*. It may be held *necessary* to the divine purpose to create a world where moral evil is *possible* but then it may be said that suffering is a *contingency* that has come about by the human actualization of a divinely given possibility, so that the necessity of suffering cannot be ascribed directly to the divine purpose as such. But even if Bauckham's point requires significant reformulation here it may leave intact the gravamen of the response to the theodicy issue which is positively set forth by, *e.g.,* Moltmann. And that is really our present concern.

Moltmann gives hope in a suffering world from a perspective of eschaton and cross; in short, we have *eschatologia crucis*.[8] The promise of the plerosis of divine presence in the future and the event of the kenosis of divine being in the past not only buoy up the heart but stimulate praxis. There are many welcome features of Moltmann's proposal, including the governing aspiration to order theological reflection to the missionary task without tumbling into shallow pragmatism. The proposal is also far wider ranging than indicated above, embracing the ambition of reworking Christian theology as a trinitarian *eschatologia salutis*, as the work developed.[9] I waive here consideration of these things. Rather, we focus on certain critical questions that emerge from Moltmann's discussion. As we do so, we bear in mind that giving hope in a suffering world entails exchanging the studies of the academies for the sobrieties of the actualities; those who emphasize both the historical location and historical responsibility of theology definitely have some purchase on the truth of the matter here.

The plain man, or at any rate the plain theologian, will want to ask: what is hope? And a plain reply from the least plain of

---

7. See the brief account by K. Surin, *Theology and the Problem of Evil,* Oxford, 1986.

8. A phrase used in the very first major work, *A Theology of Hope,* III.4.

9. Especially in *The Trinity and the Kingdom of God,* London, 1981.

thinkers, Soren Kierkegaard, is: hope is 'the passion for the possible'. Leaving aside Kierkegaard's rich intricacies it is good to take seriously both the passion and the possibility in hope. It is plentifully passionate: it clings, even against hope and, as with faith, its object is *pinned*. To trifle with people's hopes is no trifling thing. 'Hope deferred makes the heart sick' says the author of Proverbs (13:12) who was not prone to emotive exaggeration in any matters, including matters of the heart. And to defer is not to abolish; it is to stretch out but not infinitely surrender.[10] Disappointment is more bitter than deferring for it may entail realistic abandonment of the object. Paul was no trifler either when in a tranquillising understatement he tells us that hope does not disappoint us (Romans 5:15).[11] Disappointments only matter much when passion is around.

The category of 'possibility' too is stabley allied with the concept 'hope'. Hope is oriented to the future; the future is not certain; enter possibility, whether or not of Kierkegaardian brand. In its sober moments, hope admits that its certainties are spurious but passion and sobriety take time to be bedfellows in the heart. If hope ought to be sustained it ought not to be sustained by implicating assurance. Hope is ordered to the possible, a possibility it establishes by extrapolation or imagination without knowing whether it will break the surface of actuality.[12]

That is one facet of hope, but is it one facet of *Christian* hope? Christian hope is a passion too but a passion, as Moltmann indeed reminds us, for what is *promised*. Indeed, it is kindled specifically by this, according to Moltmann's first attempts to dwell on it.[13] Since the promise is, or is believed to be, divine, it should not lead to a dangerous hope or a hope

10. See commentaries on Proverbs here *ad loc., e.g.*, D. Kidner, *Proverbs*, Leicester, 1964.
11. Despite the occasional proposal to the contrary, it is surely wrong to expand the reference of this verse to human hopes in general. See C. E. B. Cranfield, *Romans I-VIII*, Edinburgh, 1975, *ad loc.*
12. The terms and metaphor here are borrowed from Bloch and Moltmann; see Bauckham, *Moltmann*, ch. 1.
13. For an important comment on the difficulties of this, see R. Alves, *A Theology of Human Hope*, New York, 1969, pp. 56-68.

which is an admixture of curse and blessing.[14] It cannot be disappointed and thus is not stayed on the possible if by *possible* we mean that which is not objectively assured. It is true that this requires defence in theological, let alone other, circles these days but *Moltmann* will not charge us with any significant error here. His promise is the promise which, *qua* divine, is eschatologically infallible and he insists that it creates possibilities for proximate, anticipatory actualization in the world.[15] But what is obscured in his analysis when giving hope to *others*[16] is that some difference attaches to the passions kindled by promise and those kindled by possibility respectively. Self–knowledge of potential disappointment ought usually to qualify passionate hope for the *promised* would be ignorance, not knowledge. Hope for the possible may arise *from* hope for the promise and arise *instead of* despair but it is not that passion which Paul joined with faith and charity.

So what? This: unless one sustains the distinction in relation to the passions of the human spirit, one may give false hope to the suffering.[17] To impart hope is sometimes to impart a blessing; to want to impart it is usually a well–meaning instinct. But lest it turn into a curse it must sometimes be checked. People are often encouraged to hope for recovery from illness and to identify their hope with faith, the substance of things hoped for. Then they decline and add bewilderment to burden; they die and thus is added despair to the grief of those who shared the hope. Assuredly, all this implies a perspective on God and physical healing which I am simply assuming and not defending here. But the assumption is for the purposes of illustration. At least for Moltmann and

14. Contrast the legend of Pandora's box, of which there is more than one version. Useful references are given in H. U. von Balthasar, *Truth is Symphonic,* 1987, pp. 171-173.
15. So while the end of history is not an open question, for God has given a promise, history is open to its end.
16. Note how he distinguishes between the immediate and the profounder hope when recording his own war-time experience. See M. D. Meeks, *Origins of the Theology of Hope,* Philadelphia, 1979, pp. xf.
17. Peter's 'living hope' (I Peter 1:3) is implicitly the antithesis of false hope as well as of living hopelessness.

doubtless the majority of theologians in his broad circle the assumption is valid.

But if our question is now whether in giving hope to a suffering world we may at times be accentuating, not attenuating, suffering, is the *illustration* valid? *Prima facie* it falters on the failure to distinguish between diseases of the body physical and diseases of the body politic. After all, the battle with physical ill is the battle with *nature* in the cases I have implicitly in mind; whatever the humanly controllable element in disease that gives the battle its distinctive shape. But that is not the case with social ill and here we have in mind the far too generalized but nevertheless identifiable situation of poverty and oppression which Moltmann so often has in mind. Here, our strife is with *systems* managed by *persons* in the cases explicitly in his mind. Indeed, it may be pressed that it is precisely the ascription to social order of a similar kind of inevitability as we ascribe to the natural order that has cruelly hampered social reform.

The distinction here is certainly valid, but its validity does not dispel the validity of the illustration. If we *pin* our hopes on social change, adopting a passion generated precisely by the pinning, we can experience the setbacks, frustration and despair of the physically afflicted by bodily malfunction. So when theologians laud the merits of a hopeful disposition and hopeful activity it is the distinction between the promised and the possible, not the social and the impersonal, that must be in mind. Yet the relevant distinction is tacit to the point of obscurity in much contemporary theological writing on hope.[18] Why? There may be a number of reasons. But one may surmise that a governing one is the fear that the end of this road is the restriction of any profound hope to a transcendent beyond or qualitatively new (and perhaps remotely distant) future ... and once that happens social concern will die a quiet death.

18. One may be challenged to plough through the immense amount of literature on hope in our generation to see how often the distinction is cleanly or prominently made. Yet, of course, awareness of the distinction is present and often crops up, as it could hardly fail to do in a theological generation that knows the neo-orthodoxy of Barth *et al.*

This fear is understandable but it should be allayed. One should be willing to take the consequences of the distinction between hopes as they lodge themselves in the human heart, but the consequences are not quietistic indifference. This is so for two reasons. First, there may be compelling reasons for the activity often assigned to hope that are untouched by the distinction of hopes. I think there are, the foundational command to love God and neighbour being supreme.[19] Secondly, the 'possible' should stand contrasted with the 'impossible', not just with the 'assured'. Whatever the ramifications of Moltmann's early metaphysical commitments[20] or even the precise connection between resurrection and promise in his theology[21] the proposition that the world is open to divine transforming activity in its temporal course is surely secure and in fact one might wish to specify divine *ordinations* for such transformations.[22] Banally truistic as this may sound in some theological ears, it opens the way for the removal of fears of indifference; further, if the driving passion of the Christian is the accomplishment of the will of God, one must establish a *unity*, not just a *distinction* within the passion for the *possible* and for the *promised*, for in both cases we press on to strive and obey in accordance with God's beckoning whatever the realtion may be between temporal and eschatological fulfilments.[23] If we keep these

19. The point cannot be argued here but for a useful survey of the pertinent biblical material see S. C. Mott, *Biblical Ethics and Social Change,* Oxford, 1982.
20. One thinks here of the influence of Bloch, less overt in the later writing.
21. In *Theology of Hope, passim,* Moltmann envisages some sort of 'process', never given extended treatment, between resurrection and eschaton.
22. The accent, of course, is heavily on freedom not on divine ordination in contemporary theology and even allowing for concepts of freedom not greatly connected with the traditional freedom / foreordination discussion, the underlying rivalries persist.
23. The passion to do the will of God, intelligent as it undoubtedly must be, arguably suffices without knowledge of how the temporal and eschatological are related, for purposes of vigorously prosecuting a course of action. For a somewhat different slant, however, which must command considerable sympathy, see the third part of Oliver

two reasons in mind we may share with all, including all the suffering, the great hope of eschatological salvation[24] and give more particular hopes strictly as particular situations are presented to us where people suffer and God bids us strive on their behalf.

But let us turn now to Moltmann's theology of the cross. It is, as the phrase suggests, the deliberate adoption of an insight of Luther's though how far it is consistent with Luther's own *theologica crucis* another matter.[25] *The Crucified God* remains the most compelling and comprehensive exposition of the way in which the cross gives hope to the suffering where the *theeologia crucis* is developed intentionally as social criticism. The Christ of this cross is the blasphemer who proclaimed grace and not law, the agitator who communicated an alternative politics.[26] These roles suffice to make their impression on those who suffer, particularly when the unity of life and death is taken into account. Here there may be fellowship. But what *disunites* life and gives rise to the most puzzling feature of the cross for Moltmann's Saviour is especially the one who proclaimed God's nearness in his life but experienced forsakenness in death. 'My God, my God why have you forsaken me?' (Mark 15:34). Moltmann thinks that the answer to this cry enables us to give hope from the cross to a suffering world. Two things can be said here, both of which achieve that revolution in the

---

O'Donovan's *Resurrection and Moral Order*, Leicester, 1986, in relation to the argument of the whole work.

24. The present writer would wish to understand this as a commitment to belief in continued personal existence beyond the grave but not to belief in universal salvation.

25. As surely as Luther could cite Isaiah 45.15 *(Vere tu es deus absconditus)* he could emphasise the prophetic diagnosis *(. . . Iniquitates vestrae . . . et peccata vestra absconderunt faciem eius a vobis,* Isaiah 59.2). Despite his extremely complimentary references to Moltmann, Alister McGrath's own work raises the obvious question to ask on the basis of Luther's thought, namely, to what extent Moltmann does or can detach a Lutheran *theologia crucis* from a Lutherian *iustitia Dei* in its material content? See McGrath, *Luther's Theology of the Cross*, Oxford, 1985, pp. 159, 180.

26. Moltmann expounds this, whether felicitously or not, in *The Crucified God*, ch. 4.

concept of God which a contemporary theodicy is bound to propose.[27]

First, God is passible. The axiom of impassibility, which has fuelled the fires of protest atheism, must be dropped. This is a break with classical theism which, while allowing for mitigating circumstances in this matter, is an albatross, as several contemporaries have felt. Theopaschitism does not reduce to Patripassianism: in the case of 'the crucified God',[28] while the Son suffers unto death, the Father suffers unto the death of the Son. It is thus better to speak of death in God than the death *of* God. If the Son suffered godforsakenness and death, then the suffering know that God has experienced their condition. This does not only put an important perspective on suffering; it means that the atheist protest against a God of omnipotent impassibility is justified from the cross.

Secondly, this is soteriologically decisive. Father and Son are united in their deep separation and from the event of the cross flows the life–giving Spirit. Moltmann thus interprets, in one of the most distinctive of his theological moves, the cross of Christ in trinitarian terms. The Spirit which flowed out of the event of the death of the Son in God gives life to a needy world so that the entire history of the world is now taken up with its hopes and its sufferings into the history of God. This Spirit is, indeed, suspiciously Hegelian if one finds Hegel suspicious.[29] But the point in any event is to blot

27. As Moltmann argues especially in the central chapter of his work, itself named *The 'Crucified God'*.

28. Jüngel is certainly right to note Tertullian's use of the phrase here, if Moltmann really did hold the phrase as such to be original to the late Middle Ages; see E. Jüngel, *God as the Mystery of the World*, Edinburgh, 1983, p. 65. See, too, Bauckham, *Moltmann*, p. 157 (10). Yet, clearly something great is going on here with Luther's use of the term; see McGrath, *op. cit.* pp. 1, 146.

29. I am in substantial agreement here with Bauckhan's cautious allowance that an Hegelian reading of *The Crucified God* is 'perhaps the most obvious' at this point (Bauckham, *Moltmann*, p. 107). It is, I think, less the kind of economic trinitarianism we have here that suggests this than Moltmann's failure, in any criticisms of Hegel, to distance himself from Hegel's understanding of the relation of divine mind to matter, though Moltmann clearly eschews a Marxian

out the picture of the Trinity as an eternal, self–contained fellowship, a circle that hovers like a halo over the world. The Trinity is the dynamic relationship of Father, Son and Spirit unfolding in time, through history, and so doing not apart from human history but by taking up that history into the life of God, the history of God. Our suffering unto death happens 'in God'.[30] And as for hope? God's destiny is to be at home in his own world where he will one day be all in all in the kingdom of freedom and righteousness. Suffering will be transformed into eschatological victory. So God is *with* us when we suffer and *before* us as One pledged to bring the world to its eschatological transformation.

Both these things imply a criticism of society. God in the cross sides with the poor, the oppressed, the rejected, the godforsaken as we see largely in the life of Jesus too. A social and political order which took that seriously would be challenged to its foundations. We must openly charge society with forgetfulness of the crucified God; further, we must labour to change it by exposing its false values and actively participating in the history of God who will eschatologically overcome all ills in his kingdom of righteousness.

So we do not just suffer, we challenge; we do not just challenge, we work; we do not just work, we hope. We are back where we started earlier in this essay.

There is certainly room for the claim that God is passible and for Moltmann's attempt to tackle theodicy not by arguing in justification of God but by describing his ways, past, present and future. As with much else in his work I here pass over features of it which seem to me to be fundamentally plausible. But there are other features that require critical comment. And the one here selected is the fate of the doctrine of the atonement.

---

materialism. *Cf.* W. Panneberg, 'What is Truth?',, in *Basic Questions in Theology*, II, London, 1971, pp. 1-27, Here, despite Pannenberg's claim that dubbing Hegel pantheist is mistaken, it says much for his view of the Hegelian concept of God that the really serious defect in Hegel is 'that the horizon of the future is lost'. (p. 22)

30. Moltmann refers to his theology as 'dynamic panentheism'; Bauckham, *Moltmann* has a helpful exposition of related points in ch. 4.

Quite what that fate is may be open for legitimate discussion. It has been bluntly suggested that Moltmann lacks such a doctrine.[31] The basis of this charge, as Alan Lewis makes it, is the opposition to expiation which Moltmann evinces in his discussion in *The Crucified God.*[32] The matter is not quite so secure, however, for a number of reasons, amongst them Moltmann's habit of apparently denying in one place what he apparently partially allows elsewhere[33] (the word 'not' slides uneasily into 'not only' occasionally in his literature) and his undoubted emphasis on justification with its connection with guilt and necessary connection with the cross.[34] What *is* the case is that little positive attention is paid by Moltmann to that aspect of atonement theology that has shaped the distinctive tradition stemming in the West from Anselm and the magisterial Reformers.[35] Now it may be

---

31. Most recently in a striking essay by Professor Alan Lewis, 'The Burial of God: Rupture and Resumption as the Story of Salvation', in *Scottish Journal of Theology*, 40.3, 1987, pp. 335-362, p. 352 n. 33.
32. Pp. 181ff.
33. See the statement: 'Christ did not die *only* as that expiatory offering in which the law was restored . . .' (p. 186). This is a somewhat unexpected statement (italics are mine) not only in relation to what has just been said about expiation but, indeed, the law, in this work.
34. See the essay, 'Justification and the New Creation, in The Future of Creation', ch. x, London, 1979. Here, justification, guilt and cross are connected but the accent is on the end of the works of God which has to do with the triumph of the new creation over nothingness. The important issue that arises here really comes under the heading: incarnation as the fulfilment of creation, not just for the sake of redemption. Very broadly, Moltmann wishes to follow the Scotist-Barthian tradition in affirming this over against the Anselmian one. Anselm enters *The Crucified God* only in this connection (pp. 260, 288). For some related criticisms which take up some of the themes in *Future of Creation* see Douglas Schuurmann, 'Creation, Eschaton and Ethics: an Analysis of Theology and Ethics' in Jurgen Moltmann in *Calvin Theological Journal* 22.1, 1987, pp. 42-67. Note, in the essay I have cited from *The Future of Creation*, the negative reference to expiation, p. 163.
35. One should not flatten this out, of course. But I include Luther in this tradition: see Paul Althaus, *The Theology of Martin Luther*, Philadelphia, 1966, pp. 218-223, persuasively *pace* Aulen.

argued that Moltmann does not need to give this area much positive consideration as his avowed aim is to develop a *theologia crucis* not completely comprehensively but as social criticism.[36] This is a possible, though I think doubtful defence.[37] But let us ask positively: what would a *theologia crucis* which highlighted the traditional concern to connect guilt and suffering[38] at the cross contribute, if anything, to the gift of hope in a suffering world?

First one must, parallel with hope, stress that in the cross which meets the universal conditions of humankind. It is paradoxically the case that when we stress our theological and practical concern for the *suffering,* the sufferers themselves may get lost in the crowd.[39] This is so for two reasons. First, the 'poor and oppressed' are lumped together as a homogeneous group in some ways[40] whereas starvation, poverty and lack of democratic freedom are not the same thing and variation in the causes and circumstances of poverty, for instance, means corresponding social variety. Secondly, in the revolt against false individualism it may be easily forgotten that serious concern for the suffering is grounded in the capacity to enter into the circumstances of the individual,[41] whose suffering is not proportionately increased or decreased by his membership of a mathematically calculable company who may be similarly suffering. Indeed, this latter point is important for the way the theodicy issue takes shape, for the

36. See the preface to *The Crucified God.*
37. The reason is partly indicated by what has been said about expiation. The omissions of chapter 2 of *The Crucified God* appear significant in this respect.
38. See Lewis, *op. cit.* p. 352. Lewis acquits Jüngel of the charge he brings against Moltmann by referring to law and substitution in Jüngel. For Moltmann's comments on substitution, see *The Crucified God,* p. 263. *Cf.* the reference here to 'alienation' in the context of Soelle's work with my comments below.
39. Though he does not develop it along the same lines, this instinct broadly informs Surin's whole treatment, too, *op. cit.*
40. As with 'hope', Moltmann does offer distinctions but they are not always prominent at all.
41. One recalls the epistolary counsel of Che Guevara to one of his family or intimates, to have always the capacity to feel deeply for any afflicted by injustice.

way that statistics are given can give the impression that there is a *quantum* of suffering related to the *number* of those who suffered as though the earthquake that kills a hundred has caused *correspondingly* more suffering than the one which kills ten.[42] While I shall not pursue it here, it seems to me that this provokes serious thought on the question of God's suffering: is it not he who has the capacity to suffer *with each individual,* and is it not God, therefore, who truly suffers on account of the sheer *accumulation* of suffering in the world?

To return, however, to the connection between guilt and suffering, let us remember that those who suffer social deprivation in some form also frequently feel the weight of guilt. An act of cruelty to father or son; a rash word that plunged another into needless trouble; the cowardice that increased another's distress; the piece of bread stolen from one's fellow-prisoner[43] – these incur guilt. All this can plague the conscience of one already suffering physical or social deprivation. Here it is the word of the cross, the word of forgiveness, the word that tells of an atoning sacrifice for sin that deals with the suffering of the guilty. To speak of such things is to affirm, not to denigrate, their humanity – it is to treat them as persons in a world cruelly treating them as non-persons.[44] Because the sufferer is also God's creature, not just man's victim, the cross speaks of guilt in the midst of suffering too.

Are we now guilty of showing a callous interest in people's guilt when their bodies are racked with pain and minds permanently clouded by deep anxiety? Such callousness would indeed be without excuse. Thomas Hanks has

---

42. *Cf.* on this in particular C. S. Lewis, *The Problem of Pain*, London, 1940, ch. vii, proposition 5.
43. On father and son, see Wiesel's oft-quoted story (*e.g.*, in Surin, *op. cit.* 121, and Bauckham, *Theodicy*, p. 88); on bread, see R. Wurmbrand, *Sermons in Solitary Confinement*, 1969, p. 17, and see A. Solzhenitsyn, *One Day in the Life of Ivan Denisovich*, Hammersmith, 1963, pp. 110-143.
44. See C. S. Lewis again for what will strike some as a counter-intuitive argument with a family resemblance to mine, that only a retributive understanding of punishment truly establishes human dignity and advances human rights *in the case of the individual concerned* in *Undeceptions*, London, 1971, 111.4.

remarked that 'the Reformers . . . could proclaim bluntly "all have sinned" and never ask themselves how incoherent, absurd or irrelevant that might sound to beings that view themselves as one more pig in the trough. . . .'[45] Hanks is criticising neither the Reformers nor their theology. What he is saying he is saying to those of us who wish to share and apply the Reformers' and Bible's Gospel in circumstances such as obtain in Latin America, where he works.[46] It appears to me that we must take his words to heart and develop them by considering the different kinds of suffering in today's world. So the implication of the reference to guilt and suffering is no more that we dismiss other kinds of suffering than the implication of delimiting and defining hope was that we become socially indifferent.

If this is understood, a further point may be made. Our implicit understanding of the atonement involves, of course, belief in the *uniquely* redemptive sufferings of Jesus Christ. It has been argued that such belief, particularly in the context of the question of suffering, is fatally alienating. The word 'alienating' in modern theology is rich in connotation not only of atonement theologies but also of social philosophies and in particular it brings to mind Marx's critical deployment of Hegelian concepts and constructive development of his own *Weltanshaung*. In the present context, the charge is that uniquely redemptive suffering severs the world of God's transactions from the world of human misery by dissociating the sufferers of the Son from those of the created family.[47] What are we to make of this charge?

We read of Jesus that he underwent some of the things that other sufferers have had to undergo – betrayal, misrepresentation, mockery, violence. Those who suffer know better than those who do not how important for them that is. One must, however, ask the question: is it the case that the one who most effectively imparts strength, comfort,

---

45. 'The Evangelical Witness to the Poor and Oppressed' in *TSF Bulletin* (September-October, 1986), quotation from p. 13.
46. Hanks is classed by D. W. Ferm as a liberation theologian: *Third World Liberation Theologies: an Introductory Survey*, 1986, p. 51f.
47. See Dorothee Soelle's bitter work, *Suffering*, London, 1975, though I do not mean to deliver a purely negative judgment on this work.

hope and love to those who suffer is someone who has similarly suffered and on the basis of that can impart blessing? The answer is often: 'yes'. But not always. When a person loves deeply, sorrows with our sorrows, rejoices in our joy, *that* person has the ability to communicate strength. But sheer reflection on experience, particularly of pastoral experience, will show that the contingent fact that the comforter has not suffered in the particular ways involved has not in the least put him or her at a relative disadvantage, not, that is, *necessarily*. No-one loved or sorrowed as did Jesus, nor so laid down his life in sorrow and love. Grasped properly, awareness of the depth of love involved in the atoning sacrifice gives more succour to the sufferer than do even those sufferings common to Jesus and his fellow-men.

However, I have shifted from 'giving hope' to 'giving strength' and this may appear to confirm suspicions that the spectre of quietism (or some such thing – spectres are not easily named) hovers over the discussion. We have, after all, not affirmed Moltmann's contention that the cross is protest, active protest, against suffering. It is certain that we should interpret the concept of 'protest' here in the precise form and with the precise connotations given by Moltmann for it is associated with some pretty debased jangle some of the time for some of us who observe the public face of contemporary Western democracy. By and large, as Moltmann applies his theology in, *e.g.*, the closing chapters of *The Crucified God*, there is probably not anything fundamentally objectionable about its ramifications as he pits the way of the cross in the public arena against lords many who certainly do not care to make their world cruciform. The initial point must be remembered, that our purpose in this essay is not to stress points of agreement. Having said this, we will allow the spectre one more brief sortie before reaffirming our desire to banish him (or her?) perpetually.

If cross, hope and suffering come together to impose their mark on any one canonical writing, it is undoubtedly in Peter's first letter. It is not surprising to find that this piece, along with the letter to the Hebrews, is the most problematic for theologians of liberation.[48] It *is* noteworthy that despite the clearly distinctive place 'hope' has in I Peter (it 'shows more compellingly than almost any other New Testament writing what strong moral stimulus hope gives'[49]) its author has not made much of a hit with Moltmann, either. Without entering exegetical or theological detail[50] – the suffering are called to endure and this is the light both of the cross that stood on the earth and the inheritance that awaits in heaven. Indeed, it would be irresponsible to assume too much what this has to say to our theme without specifying what kind of suffering is involved here and what may be inferred from it. Further, the hermeneutical task accomplishes a vital mediation between the text and its contemporary application here which further disposes us to treat its *prima facie* witness circumspectly.[51] Having said that, the letter simply stamps indelibly on our minds what the rest of the New Testament also testifies: that in particular cases the greatest thing and worthiest that the cross and the hope can do for the suffering is to enable endurance and even submission.[52] If we do not say this as we try to give hope in a suffering world, we will too often discover by experience what we did not receive in faith, that the exorcism of one heartless and soulless social demon just leads to a regrouping of demons and a return invasion.

At this point we note afresh what has been evident from the outset, that theological reflection is badly cramped in such questions as we have treated by addressing these questions at

48. I owe confirmation of this to a remark once made in a public meeting by Thomas Hanks.
49. R. Schnackenburg, *The Moral Teaching of the New Testament*, London, 1965, p. 368.
50. In particular one should not assume that suffering is a homogeneous experience in this epistle nor that Petrine eschatology is a pure spiritualisation of Old Testament promises (see commentaries *ad loc.*).
51. See on this generally L. Goppelt, *Theology of the New Testament*, vol. 2, Grand Rapids, 1982, pp. 161ff, and brief closing remarks by E. Cothenat, *Le Realisme de l'Esperance Chretienne selon 1 Pierre* in *New Testament Studies* 27.4), July 1981, pp. 564-571, despite the rather bland tone of the article.
52. Note the comment here by Goppelt, *op. cit.*, p. 168.

a level of relative abstraction. If abstraction is not to turn into speculative luxury it must not only be slow to speak, but swift to stop speaking. Then it will hear the cries of those to whom God would make himself known as Father. And more eloquent than reflection will be the haste with which it moves to give hope in a suffering world.

MORAL REASON IN HISTORY:
AN ESSAY IN DEFENCE OF CASUISTRY

Nigel Biggar

It is commonly accepted that one of the distinguishing marks of the cultural type that we call modernity is 'historical consciousness'. By this, of course, we do not mean that modern culture is the first to be possessed of a simple awareness of the past. Nor, when we describe historical consciousness as 'modern', do we intend by it an acknowledgement of the *dependence* of the present upon the past, of the debt owed by us to our forebears, of the value of tradition. In that sense, modern culture may be typified by the deliberate pursuit of historical oblivion.

In fact, however, 'modern' culture has never been more than partly modern. Modernity has never existed in pure form. So, while we in the Western world of the 1980s think of ourselves as modern and identify ourselves as those who have broken with the *ancien régime*, and while we manage our personal and social lives with a heavy presumption in favour of change and novelty, we nevertheless betray a measure of cultural neurosis in our passion for historical drama, in our apparent tendency as consumers to prefer whatever is marketed as 'traditional', and especially if we are from the New World, in our assessment of social status largely in terms of the strength of our association with the old one. We who pretend to be modern are by no means above joining our less progressive predecessors in admiring an idealised past.[1]

Nevertheless, when we distinguish modern consciousness as 'historical', we are not speaking vacuously. We are saying something significant. We are saying that one of the legacies of the European Enlightenment has been a heightened sensi-

---

1. See the discussion of this paradoxical relationship by the eminent American sociologist, Edward Shils, in the introduction to his book, *Tradition* (Chicago: University of Chicago Press, 1981). Historical association as a socially elevating force in contemporary American society is one of the themes of Paul Fussell's book on social status in the United States, *Class* (New York: Ballantine, 1984) – published under the title *Caste Marks* in the United Kingdom (London: Heinemann, 1984).

tivity to the *historicity* of human custom and institution and understanding. To be possessed of an 'historical' consciousness in this sense means to be quite acutely sensitive to the fact that all of our beliefs are conditioned by the combination of time and place in which we believe them. It is to be highly aware of historical and cultural relativity. Modern culture is certainly not the first to possess such an awareness: the Sophists of the Ancient World were hardly lacking in it. But modern culture is widely reckoned to be distinctive in the measure to which this particular sensitivity has come to dominate cultural consciousness.

An awareness of the historical relativity of human understanding might be developed into the metaphysical conviction that there are no permanent or absolute truths; that human beliefs are exhausted by their relations to a particular time and place. An awareness of historical relativity, that is to say, might degenerate into the dogma of historical relativism. But it need not. And our concern with historical consciousness will not be with the question of whether or not there are absolute truths – important though that question is; but, rather, simply with issues raised by consciousness of the historical relativity of human understanding.

This consciousness involves an awareness of the ways in which the historical situation, our place in time, informs our apprehension of truth. But note that 'historical situation' here does not simply refer to one's social or cultural environment. Heideggerian hermeneutics has served us well in drawing our attention to the way in which our understanding is informed, not just by what surrounds us, but by what we have become; that is, by the histories that we represent. We do not perform acts of understanding or interpretation as absolute Cartesian egos. Our consciousnesses do not confront the world as *tabulae rasae*. When we seek to understand or interpret, we do so with pre-understandings formed in particular and peculiar ways by our genetic inheritance, our experience, our past decisions, our fears and loves, our convictions and prejudices. The historical situation is not simply external to the one who would understand. It includes the history of the interpreter himself.

Nor, according to Liberation theology, is one's historical situation simply a matter of consciousness; it is partially –

according to Liberation theologians, primarily – a matter of his political commitment. When one seeks to understand, he does not do so in a political vacuum. He does so either committed to defend the political *status quo* (or, at least, to see it defended) or committed to change it. There is no neutral position. And one's inevitable political commitment, whether tacit or explicit, will shape (some would say, determine) the questions one asks and does not ask, what one pays attention to and what one neglects, what one regards as important and what as trivial.

So far, so good; but not far enough. For, political commitment is not different in kind from all the other commitments that one makes. Whenever one invests oneself, whenever one acquires an interest – whether economic, social, professional, moral, philosophical – he adds to his view of the world a certain bias. What we see depends heavily upon what we care for. There is every reason, therefore, why the hermeneutical function that Liberation theologians ascribe to the political investment of the self should be extended to all forms of self-investment. The historical situation in which understanding or interpretation takes place should be so conceived as to embrace all kinds of praxis.

We have spoken of historical consciousness as an awareness of the historicity of human understanding; of its relativity to the historical situation in which it occurs, whether this be social and cultural environment, personal history or various species of praxis. There is another, second dimension of modern historical consciousness which we must attend to: the unique particularity of the historical situation, even when that situation is morally significant. Acutely aware of history as a process, not of repetition, but of change, historical consciousness recognises that there is an irreducible element of novelty in each morally significant situation and that, therefore, the mechanical application of traditional rules cannot be a fitting way of making a response to it. Adding to such a concept of history a combination of historicist confidence in the human capacity for beneficent reform, a Romantic belief in creative genius and an existentialist concept of authenticity, this consciousness understands moral decisions, not as acts of conformity to a given law, but as unique, decisive and creative ventures.

IN DEFENCE OF CASUISTRY

It is arguable that the contemporary consciousness of the West is a composite, not only of modern and pre-modern elements, but of post-modern ones, too. After the political failures and horrors of the 20th century, our historicist confidence is not what it was; and we are, perhaps, a little more appreciative both of the extent to which even creative ventures depend upon tradition, and of the extent to which even authentic, decisive individuals need the support of a community. Still, we are no more simply post-modern than we were ever simply modern. If our confidence in the human capacity to engineer a better world has been chastened, it still lives on – at least because we have no confidence in other means of achieving the absolute material security that we pursue. And if we have rediscovered some of the virtues of tradition and community, we still remain fiercely attached to the ideal of individual autonomy, especially in matters of 'private' morals, tellingly so-called. It seems safe, then, to say that the consciousness of Western culture in the 1980s is substantially 'historical', not only in its sensitivity to the formative impact of the historical situation upon understanding that occurs within it; but also in its normative concept of the making of a moral decision as a unique, creative act, ultimately free of regulation.

It should not be surprising that one of the ethical casualties of the emergence of this two-fold historical consciousness has been casuistry. This is most clear in the case of Roman Catholic moral theology where, under the liberalizing influence of Vatican II, there has been a reaction against what has been held to be the rigid, deductive rationalism of the casuistic tradition. Charles Curran, for example, noting in 1968 that Roman Catholic moral theology was becoming more 'historically conscious', prophesied a widespread reaction against 'excessive rationalism' according to which reason was supposed 'to solve all the complicated moral problems with clear and definite answers'.[2] In Protestant circles, it is true that casuistry perished suddenly at the end of the seventeenth century, some two centuries before we can speak confidently

---

2. Charles E. Curran, 'Absolute Norms in Moral Theology' in Gene H. Outka & Paul Ramsey, eds., *Norm and Context in Christian Ethics* (New York: Scribner's, 1968), pp. 171-72.

of the presence of modern historical sensibility. But if Kenneth Kirk is correct in attributing its demise partly to the rise of Pietism,[3] then we may surmise that it was connected with the Pietist reaction against rationalism in its Lutheran scholastic form. We do, therefore, have ground for supposing that the kind of concern that led to the disappearance of Protestant casuistry in the late 17th century was not entirely unlike that which has led to the abandonment of casuistry by Roman Catholics in the late 20th.

It is not the case, of course, that historical consciousness alone bears responsibility for contemporary disaffection for casuistry. Close to the heart of much Protestant (especially Lutheran) sensibility lies a basic suspicion of law and legal procedures, nourished by a tendency to associate these with soteriological legalism; that is, the belief that eternal salvation is achieved by observance of the moral law. Many Protestants – the Puritans obviously excepted – have also tended to be supicious of too close an attention to being and doing what is right, since it is supposed to conduce to an anxious conscience and therefore the lapse of faith. Further, Protestants have been possessed of an anti-authoritarian streak, which expresses itself in a restriction of sacerdotal authority and the championing of the liberty of the individual conscience. All of these characteristics have contributed to Protestant alienation from casuistry, a kind of moral reasoning which is undoubtedly legal in form; has certainly been used with legalistic intention; and was for a long time, in the Roman Catholic tradition, the means by which priests reached a verdict on the appropriate penance with which to sentence a confessed sinner. Moreover, much of what has been characteristic of Protestantism from the beginning, is now also characteristic of those Roman Catholic circles sympathetic to the ethos of Vatican II.

There is no question, then, that the demise of casuistry in both Protestant and Roman Catholic circles has had multiple causes, only some of them functions of the emergence of historical consciousness. Nevertheless, historical consciousness, as we have defined it, has played an important, even decisive, role. One of the most common objections levelled

3. Kenneth E. Kirk, *Conscience and its Problems* (London: Longmans, Green & Co., 1927), pp. 203-4.

against casuistry in recent Christian ethics is that its mechanical rigidity prevents it from doing justice to the unique particularity of the historical situation. This is the gist of Emil Brunner's complaint that 'casuistry tries to imprison life in a net of "cases" as though all could be arranged beforehand ...';[4] that it seeks to deduce the 'case' from a general law 'in the minutest particular',[5] reckoning that 'the law in its general character logically includes within itself all particular propositions'.[6] Equivalent statements may be found in Barth, Bonhoeffer, Thielicke, Fletcher and Curran.[7] In addition to having acquired a modern sensitivity to the particularities of history, Protestantism, with its aboriginal disposition against legalism and authoritarianism and in favour of spiritual 'liberty', has sometimes warmed to elements in the existentialist concept of authentic moral decision-making; in particular, to the notion of the taking upon oneself the responsibility for launching a creative moral venture. This is most evident in the cases of Bultmann and Tillich.[8]

Recent Protestant ethics have developed further objections to casuistry of an historical nature. Paul Lehmann, for example, has accused it of abstracting the process of making moral decisions from its proper context: the history of what God is doing to humanise the world. Instead of trying 'to apply a uniform principle to a uniform or even a variegated situation', Christians should shape their action in correspondence with what God is doing in the complex and dynamic situations of

4. E. Brunner, *The Divine Imperative* (Philadelphia: Westminster Press, 1937), p. 134.
5. *Ibid.*, p. 138.
6. *Ibid.*, p. 137.
7. K. Barth, *Church Dogmatics*, III/4, ed. G. W. Bromiley & T. F. Torrance, trans. A. T. Mackay et al. (Edinburgh: T. & T. Clark, 1961), pp. 7-10; D. Bonhoeffer, *Ethics*, ed. E. Bethge (New York: Macmillan, 1955), p. 86; H. Thielicke, *Theological Ethics*, 2 vols., ed. William H. Lazarus (Grand Rapids: Eerdmans, 1979), I: 457; J. Fletcher, *Situation Ethics* (Philadelphia: Westminster, 1966), pp. 18-22, 27, 29-30; C. Curran, 'Absolutes in Moral Theology', in Outka & Ramsey, *Norm and Context*, pp. 168-9.
8. Thomas C. Oden, *Radical Obedience* (London: Epworth, 1965), pp. 25-8, 41-3, 101, 112-13; P. Tillich, *Morality and Beyond* (New York: Harper & Row, 1963), p. 42-3.

the world to bring the humanity of human beings to maturity by building up *koinonia*.[9] Lehmann also implies that casuistry has been so preoccupied with forging rational solutions to moral quandaries that it has tended to obscure the larger theological historical situation of man as sinner whom God has already acted to save.[10] Stanley Hauerwas moves along very similar lines when he criticizes casuistry (in the traditional sense) for distracting attention from the biblical story that conveys to us the theological facts of life.[11] We might fairly describe what Lehmann and Hauerwas are doing as contending against casuistry for the *theological* historicity of the moral agent. Barth's insistence that all ethical reflection be preliminary to the event of encounter between the sinful human creature and the Creator who commands in order to save – preliminary, that is, to the concrete history of God's covenantal relationship with man – intends exactly the same point.[12]

We have sought to establish that historical consciousness is, to a significant extent, responsible for discrediting casuistry as a form of moral reasoning. Conceived as a logically deductive system, moving mechanically from first principles through specific rules to particular cases, casuistry has been reckoned insensitive to the unique particularity of moral situations; inimical to moral creativity; and neglectful of the historicity – personal, social, cultural, practical, theological – of the moral agent. We shall now proceed to articulate a threefold argument: first, that Christian ethics need casuistry; second, that casuistry has suffered, particularly at Protestant hands, considerable misrepresentation; and, third, that there is a theory of casuistry that answers all of the objections presented above. In brief preface to this argument, let me make clear what it presupposes: namely, that what the above-men-

9. Paul L. Lehmann, *Ethics in a Christian Context* (New York: Harper & Row, 1963), p. 143.
10. *Ibid.*, pp. 319-22.
11. Stanley Hauerwas, *The Peaceable Kingdom* (Notre Dame: University of Notre Dame Press, 1983), pp. 117-19.
12. K. Barth, *Church Dogmatics*, II/2, ed. G. W. Bromiley and T. F. Torrance, trans. G. W. Bromiley *et al.* (Edinburgh: T. & T. Clark, 1957), pp. 676-78.

tioned historical objections wish to affirm about the historicity and creativity of moral understanding is valid; and that, therefore, the task before us is to satisfy, not to refute, them.

The alternatives offered instead of casuistic reasoning are various. Barth proposes the event of hearing God's command, albeit one informed by a measure of ethical reflection.[13] Brunner and Bonhoeffer make similar proposals;[14] though Brunner veers away from Barth and toward Fletcher in his readiness to identify directly the content of the divine command as love for God and neighbour.[15] Fletcher offers us the discernment of what is loving; Lehmann, the discernment of what is humanising; and Hauerwas, the imaginative discernment of correspondence between the biblical narrative and our own situations.[16]

All of these proposals share a reluctance to specify their norm – whether it be the divine command, love, humanity or the biblical narrative – in terms of moral rules. They leave the connexion between norm and case vague on principle, because they want to carve out a sphere of operations in Christian ethics for creative, imaginative freedom; and because they believe that this requires the exclusion of casuistry. But the refusal to specify the norm in terms of at least provisional rules, means that we are left without any tightly defined criteria by which to guide or discipline or make accountable our moral intuitions and the productions of our moral imaginations. We are left too much to our own spontaneous devices. How do I know that this command is a command of God? And by what common measure do I allow you to assess my claim to have heard one? You say that what you are doing is loving because it conduces to the greatest well-being of the most people. But what moral content do you give well-being,

13. Barth, *Church Dogmatics*, II/2: 3-31. See Nigel Biggar, 'Hearing God's Command and Thinking about What's Right. With and Beyond Barth', in Nigel Biggar, ed., *Reckoning With Barth* (Oxford: Mowbray, 1988).

14. Brunner, *Divine Imperative*, pp. 111-21; Bonhoeffer, *Ethics*, pp. 277-85.

15. Brunner, *Divine Imperative*, pp. 112, 119.

16. Fletcher, *Situation Ethics*, pp. 134ff; Lehmann, *Ethics in a Christian Context*, p. 143; Hauerwas, *The Peaceable Kingdom*, pp. 116-30.

and how do you measure it, and within which social circle, and within what period of time? You justify your action by claiming that it corresponds to what God is doing to bring humanity to maturity. But can you tell me what you mean by mature humanity in terms sufficiently specific that I could then discern whether this action in this situation would conduce to it or not? And you appeal directly to the biblical narrative. Well, which episode? And why do you give priority to this episode rather than that one? And how do you account for the more ethically abstract parts of the Bible – the discourses on ethical subjects, and the moral codes (not to mention the casuistry)? And what is to discipline the movement of your imagination from the biblical story to your situation? Without a more specific understanding of our ethical norms, we are vulnerable, on the one hand, to the temptation to use them as the ideological cloak for self-service and, on the other, to being unable to give sufficiently precise reasons for our moral decisions. Granted that rational precision is not the be-all and end-all of Christian ethics, it is nevertheless valuable. It is valuable in that it makes the logic of our moral decisions available for assessment. Unlike the alternatives proposed, casuistry has the virtue of not resting with a general identification of the ethical norm, but of venturing the explication of that norm in terms of kinds of behaviour; that is, in terms of generic principles and increasingly specific rules. It does not leave the logic of the movement from norm to action without description.

But how can we enjoy the benefit of rational precision without offending historical consciousness? How can we deal in the currency of principles and rules and at the same time do justice to the unique particularity of historical situations, permit scope for moral creativity, and take into account the historicity of the moral agent?

We begin our response to this question by arguing that casuistry has not been fairly represented by its critics. A major tradition of casuistry has always acknowledged the unique particularity of moral cases, and therefore the necessity for a measure of moral creativity. Speaking of Roman Catholic casuistry, James Gustafson has written that 'perhaps . . . only the writers of the poorest manuals, the least nuanced and historically sophisticated have claimed that the gap between general principles and particular choices and actions could be closed by logic alone'.[17] Certainly any tendency within Roman Catholic moral theology to regard casuistry as a sheerly technical process, crushing historical particularities underfoot and denying any scope for the exercise of responsible judgement, has been checked in recent decades by the reappropriation through Thomas Aquinas of the roles of prudence and equity in the application of general principles to concrete cases.[18] There is, then, a species of casuistry with a long and distinguished pedigree that has always recognised that the final moment in moral reasoning, the moment when one is faced with deciding whether this case should be subsumed under this rule, is a moment of judgement, not inexorable logic; and it is so precisely because no matter how specific a rule one brings to bear upon a case, the rule still deals in kinds and the case in particulars.

Furthermore, this casuistic tradition has always followed Aquinas in admitting that only the first principles of moral reasoning are certain; that no set of derivate rules can possibly cover all cases; and that rare and peculiar cases will require the revision of any available set of rules.[19] It therefore permits scope for the exercise of human judgement, not only the subsumption of cases under rules, but also in the reformulation of rules themselves. Moreover, this tradition acknowledges that the relationship between moral reason and particular cases, particular historical situations, is not merely technical or mechanical; it is not simply a matter of applying rules to passive matter. On the contrary, the relationship is dynamic and di-

17. James M. Gustafson, *Protestant and Roman Catholic Ethics* (Chicago: University of Chicago Press, 1978), p. 47.
18. Aquinas, *Summa Theologica*, 2ae2ae, Qq. 47, art. 2, 3, 5; 49, art. 3; 120, art. 1; Franz Furger, 'Prudence and Moral Change',*Concilium*, 5/4 (May 1968): 62-66; Bernard Haering, 'Dynamism and Continuity in a Personalistic Approach to Natural Law', in Outka & Ramsey, eds., *Norm and Context*, pp.210-15; Bernard Haering, *Free and Faithful in Christ*, 3 vols. (Slough: St Paul Publications, 1978), I:363; Josef Fuchs, *Personal Responsibility and Christian Morality* (Washington, D.C.: Georgetown University Press, 1983), pp. 185-99.
19. Aquinas, *Summa Theologica*, 1a2ae, Qq.94, art. 4, 5, 6; 96, art. 6; 120, art. 1.

alectical. If moral rules do successfully govern the majority of cases, there remains nevertheless a minority of cases so stubborn in their dissent as to provoke reform.

Kenneth Kirk, the most notable Anglican moral theologian of this century to date, sought to recover such a dynamic form of casuistry for the Church of England. In his book, *Conscience and its Problems* (1927), he argued that, in order to be morally useful, moral principles must be partially illuminated by illustrations and examples, 'by the known instances in which it holds good; . . . by an intelligible definition, which is no more than a generalisation of known examples'. He notes, however, that these illustrations and definitions are 'apt to mislead when brought face to face with new circumstances'. It is therefore the special task of casuistry to compare the new constellation of circumstances with the old illustrations, in order to discover whether their moral resemblances so outweigh their differences as to make the same principle applicable to both. In a case where the differences predominate, the 'intelligible definition' of the relevant principle must be revised so as to take into account this new illustration of the limits of its sphere of jurisdiction.[20] Kirk contrasts this dynamic form of casuistry with its 'rigorist' counterpart, whose principal error is to regard as compromise the continuous and inevitable process of the redefinition of principles, and so to insist on the application of fixed principles to irrelevant cases. The rigorist misuses the original examples employed to illustrate the principle by failing to distinguish between the essential point in them that justifies the application of the principle, and purely accidental features that do not. 'Thus', Kirk writes, 'the law is made to bind in whole categories of cases in which it has really only partial relevance, even if it is relevant to all'.[21] It should be obvious that it is against this rigorist form of casuistry that objections of an historical sort find their mark.

Another version of the dynamic theory of casuistry appears in an article written by the American Methodist, Paul Ramsey, entitled 'The Case of the Curious Exception'. This was published in 1968 and has recently been described as speaking

20. Kirk, *Conscience and its Problems*, pp. 107-9.
21. *Ibid.*, p.121.

'the last word' on the formal questions raised in the debate about situation ethics.[22] Where Kirk speaks of principles and definitions, Ramsey speaks of norms, principles and rules; and he describes the procedure of moral reason as that of specifying ever more precisely the meaning of a given norm in terms of principles and rules, both of which define *genera* and *species*, respectively, of good and bad actions, and which are differentiated simply by their degree of specificity.[23] The subsumption of a particular case under a rule occurs on the ground of certain moral features of the case. Occasionally, there arises a case that lacks some of the features required by a rule or possesses some significant features that the rule does not. Here, the casuist must judge in the light of the ultimate norm whether to redefine the rule so as to enable it to comprehend the eccentric case, or whether to remove the case altogether from the jurisdiction of the rule under which it was initially expected to fall and place it, instead, under the jurisdiction of another. Like Kirk's, Ramsey's account of casuistry brings to the fore the dialectical nature of the relationship between moral principle and particular case. Instead of thoughtlessly designating an eccentric case 'exceptional', both leaving it outside of the available scheme of principles and rules and leaving that scheme intact, Ramsey argues that it is the role of moral reason – understood as creative, not merely technical – to bring the eccentric case under the judgement of a given ethical norm either by qualifying an old rule or inventing a new one.[24]

A third recent account of casuistry as a dynamic, creative, dialectical operation appeared in 1977, this time in the work of a moral philosopher, J. M. Brennan. In his book, *The Open Texture of Moral Judgements*, Brennan argues that moral terms are 'open-textured' in the sense that 'one cannot state the necessary and sufficient conditions for their correct

22. Oliver O'Donovan, *Resurrection and Moral Order* (Leicester: IVP, 1986), p. 196.
23. Paul Ramsey, 'The Case of the Curious Exception', in Outka and Ramsey, eds., *Norm and Context*, pp. 74-5.
24. Ramsey, 'Curious Exception', pp. 67-93.

application'.[25] Therefore a scheme of moral concepts (which may be taken as equivalent to Ramsey's principles and rules) cannot be a rigid framework, but is constantly developing in response to questions about the appropriate extension of those concepts in the light of their 'sense' or 'rationale' (which may be taken as equivalent to Ramsey's norm). Brennan therefore denies that moral reasoning is strictly deductive; and would concur with Ramsey who prefers to describe it, not as the classification or derivation of moral species, but as their evolution.[26] In other words, *pace* Brunner, it does not begin with a formulation of its major premiss in terms sufficiently exhaustive as to comprehend all possible cases in advance. Such a formulation would be impossible simply because in matters of prescience, quoting H. L. A. Hart, 'we are men, not gods'.[27] Rather, moral reasoning is a process of discovering the meaning of a given ethical 'rationale' or norm in relation to an infinite range of particular cases. Oliver O'Donovan describes this dialectical process well when he writes that 'the engagement with the case show(s) up a measure of haziness and ill-definition in our understanding of the moral priniciple; the particular act(s) as a kind of magnifying glass through which the generic appear(s) with more clarity'.[28]

It should be clear that this dialectical model of casuistry does do justice to the particularity of historical cases and acknowledges the responsibility for creative reasoning that this places upon the moral agent. But what about historicity? Does this model take due account of the relativity of moral understanding to the historical situation in which it occurs, whether this be constituted by personal history, social and cultural environment, the various species of praxis, or the theological facts of life?

It should be made clear that we have no quarrel with the notion that the one who reflects on moral cases in terms of a set of principles and rules – that is, the casuist – does so un-

25. J. M. Brennan, *The Open Texture of Moral Judgements* (London: Macmillan, 1977), p.104.
26. Ramsey, 'Curious Exception', p. 91.
27. H. L. A. Hart, *The Concept of Law* (Oxford: Clarendon Press, 1961), p. 125.
28. O'Donovan, *Resurrection and Moral Order*, p. 195.

der the conditions of historicity. His grasp of the meaning of particular principles and rules is inevitably coloured by the various dimensions of his experience. Different sets of personal, social, cultural and practical experience produce different interests, different moral sensibilities, different interpretations of principles and rules and different descriptions of cases. Kirk provides one illustration of this by way of Raymond Thamin's report of his experience of putting a series of hypothetical moral cases before a class composed largely of the children of small property-owners, and of discovering them to be 'rigorist in matters which did not touch them personally, but lax in matters concerning the duties of landlords'.[29] And Barth claimed to have found another instance in the casuistical treatment of the ethics of Sabbath observance by the Puritan, William Ames. Ames allows that divine providence may often make it necessary to keep the Sabbath in ways that differ from the rule that he lays down, but stipulates that in such cases there must be evident necessity. Such necessity, however, he never acknowledges in regard to haymaking or harvesting by farmers; while in regard to the various professional activities of doctors, surgeons, apothecaries, statesmen and soldiers, he does. Therefore, Barth judges this piece of casuistry to be 'blatantly adapted to the requirements and claims of the ruling classes'.[30] The rational procedures of casuistry evidently provide no guarantee against 'historical' bias; they do not permit moral reason to rise above history. But, then, casuistry has seldom pretended to. And, indeed, the fact that the dialectical species denies that the meaning of principles and rules is exhaustively fixed *a priori*, and affirms that concrete cases have an important formative role in the

29. Kirk, *Conscience*, p. 115n.1.
30. Barth, *Church Dogmatics*, 3/4:66. In Ames' defense it should be pointed out that his distinction between haymaking and harvesting on the one hand, and the practice of medicine or government or soldiering on the other is founded on the moral distinctions between what is necessary to secure a gain and what is necessary to avoid 'some discommodity falling out unexpectedly', and between what is necessary for oneself and what is necessary for one's neighbour or the commonwealth (*Conscience with the Power and Cases Thereof* [1639; reprint ed., Amsterdam and Norwood, N. J.: Theatrum Orbis Terrarum & Walter J. Johnson, 1975], Book V, 33: 96-97).

continuous process of its evolution, implies an acknowledgement that the history of someone's experience contributes to the meaning which he currently attaches to a given principle or rule.

Dialectical casuistry is, then, quite at ease with the notion of the personal, social, cultural and practical historicity of human apprehension of the meaning of moral principles and rules. But, insofar as it ascribes to moral cases the capacity to provoke critical reflection upon available schemes of moral reason, it denies that such historicity is absolutely determinative. The fact that the awkward features of a moral case may cause one to ask questions about the adequacy of the moral concepts that his historicity bequeaths him, means that those concepts and that historicity do not imprison him.

But what about theological historicity? Does our dialectical model meet the charge that casuistry abstracts and distracts ethics from its theological context, leading the casuist to imagine her reason to be pure and simple, rather than finite and sullied? We have just noted that dialectical casuistry presupposes on the part of the casuist a capacity for self-critical moral reflection. Now we note that this capacity itself presupposes the possession of an open disposition. I must be willing to acknowledge awkward features in moral cases, if I am to bring critical self-reflection to bear upon my moral concepts. I must be ready to have my biases, my moral sensibility interrogated. I must be prepared to think again about the meaning I attach to moral principles and rules. Pre-requisite for the operation of dialectical casuistry, therefore, is the possession and development of a certain quality of character, the virtue of openness to correction – the virtue of docility. And it is at this point that dialectical casuistry declares its contingency upon a theological context. For, the development and maintenance of an open disposition itself requires that the casuist confess that he reasons always and only as a creature, as a sinful creature, as a sinful creature whom God has graciously saved; for only such a confession can produce the delicate combination of humility, self-scepticism and confidence necessary for a readiness to learn and re-learn.

In the end, then, dialectical casuistry not only incorporates sensitivity to the historical particularity of moral cases; scope for rational creativity; acknowledgement of secular historicity

34

– personal, social, cultural, practical; and awareness of the basic context provided by theological history. In the end, it presupposes the reversal of that separation of moral and spiritual theology which took place after the Council of Trent, is reckoned responsible for the increasingly legalistic tone of subsequent Roman Catholic moral theology, and was so strongly resisted by the Caroline moralists of the Church of England.[31] For, ultimately, dialectical casuistry not only presupposes consciousness of theological historicity, but the practice of a spiritual discipline – both private and public – whereby the casuist is constantly reminded of the facts about God and humanity to which the biblical narrative witnesses, and which comprise the theological context of his moral reasoning. In the end, dialectical casuistry presupposes spiritual praxis.

---

31. H.R. McAdoo, *The Structure of Caroline Moral Theology* (London: Longmans, Green & Co., 1949), pp. 9-11.

TIME, HISTORY AND ESCHATOLOGY: AN EVALUATION OF AN ASPECT OF MBITI'S THEOLOGY

Andrew Olu Igenoza

I Introduction

Salvation-history, as understood in Biblical Theology and allied disciplines, may raise the problem of the relationship between God on the one hand; and the realm of history and nature on the other. Does God have to intervene in the affairs of men for whatever reason? Is he not rather totally remote and indifferent to history and the natural order?

However the Bible does not present us with a *Deus Remotus* who has withdrawn from his creation. rather, he is the living and active God seeking to make himself known in the world of space and time — not primarily though the repeatable events of nature but through certain unrepeatable historical events in which he acts purposively. History is not just a mere concatenation of events with no ultimate meaning but rather an arena for the mighty acts of God for the salvation of people.[1] It is this biblical emphasis on the God-given content of certain moments of history that has given rise to the linear concept of time in contradistinction to the cyclic view prevalent in the ancient world and even in present-day traditonal cultures such as we find in Africa.

Professor John S. Mbiti has argued that because traditional Africans have a cyclic view of time, time for them is a two-dimensional phenomenon consisting of a past, a present and no future in any real sense. As a result they have no ambitions and are incapable of planning. According to him the future dimension of time was only recently introduced to African peoples as a result of missionary activities and colonization. This paper attempts to counteract this thesis of Mbiti. We seek to indicate that though Africans in their traditional milieu may have a cyclic view of time, they do have a perception of the future, no matter how differently from the linear, biblical concept. We assert that though traditional Africans lack the idea of a Messiah-saviour who would come at the end of time

---

1. See *e.g.* G. B. Caird, *St Luke*, Harmondsworth, 1963, p. 47.

to usher in a new eschatological age, because the idea of the future is not lacking in their psychology, they are able to comprehend the Gospel which includes ideas like 'the Messiah' and 'the Parousia' when it is preached to them, and thus come to share in the general eschatological expectations of fellow Christians worldwide. Mbiti claims that the linear concept of time is 'Western' and that this is not the only concept of time found in the Bible. We shall first of all show therefore, that the linear concept is central to the understanding of *Heilsgeschichte*, and that therefore, the concept is primarily biblical. It is against this background that we shall elaborate on Mbiti's concept of time before concluding with a evaluation.

II Time, History, Expectation and Fulfilment in the Bible

According to the biblical concept of time and history, God's sovereign purpose moves towards a final consummation. Things do not just go on or return to the point whence they began. This is in spite of the contention of Qoheleth that 'what has been is what will be, and what has been done is what will be done'. Mbiti seeks to make theological capital out of this apparently cyclic view of time, and refers to J. Marsh to the effect that Old Testament Jews were more concerned with the *content* than the *chronology* of time.[2] But this view of Qoheleth is only peripheral to the overall biblical witness and not definitive for our purpose. Qoheleth realizes that there will be a judgement, *i.e.* an end (11:9, 12:14). The overall impression the Bible creates therefore is that there was a beginning of history, and that at God's appointed period, history will come to a close.[3] However we are reminded that the Bible stresses 'times', *i.e.* the points at which God

---

2. Eccles. 1:8-9 also 3:1-8, 15; etc. See John S. Mbiti, *New Testament Eschatology in an African Background*, London, 1978, p. 39 with references.
3. The creation narratives of Genesis chapters 1 & 2 suggest the beginning of time and history. Old Testament passages like Is. 24 and Dan. 12; and New Testament passages like Mk 13; Matt. 24; II Pet. 3; I Cor. 15:24, and much of the book of Revelation do suggest an end of history as it is presently known.

himself advances his purposes in the world.[4] Such divinely appointed 'times' in the Old Testament include creation, the call of Abraham, the Exodus, the Monarchical rule of David, and the Restoration from Babylonian Exile. But among these great moments recorded in the Old Testament we may reckon that the Exodus 'Event' was the greatest apart from the creation itself. According to John Job: 'The emergence of Noah from the ark and the emergence of Abraham from Ur both provide important preludes, and the return from exile is seen as a kind of re-enactment of the Exodus. But none of these stamps a mark of the same depth on the face of Scripture as the crossing of the sea which led to the long pilgrimage to Canaan' [5]

Israelites of the settlement period again and again looked back on this *Heiblisgeschichte* as is clearly borne out by their credal statements. For example, during the offering of the first fruits of their harvest the pious Israelite was required to confess:

> A wandering Aramean was my father; and he went down into Egypt and sojourned there few in numbers and there became a nation, great, mighty and populous. And the Egyptians treated us harshly and afflicted us, and laid upon us hard bondage. Then we cried to the Lord the God of our Fathers, and the Lord heard our voice, and saw our affliction, our toil, and our oppression: and the Lord brought us out of Egypt with a mighty hand and an outstretched arm, with great terror, with signs and wonders and brought us out into this place and gave us this land.[6]

Scholars may continue to argue the scientific or historical details about the Exodus: when did it happen, 15th century or 13th century B.C., or what exactly happened? Such details were of no moment to the Israelites. It had happened in the past, and their God had done it for their Salvation; that was enough. The importance of this Exodus episode in Israelite understanding of themselves as Yahweh's people is

---

4. M. H. Cressey, 'Time', in *The New Bible Dictionary*, London, reprinted 1975, p. 1278.
5. John Job, *The Teaching of the Old Testament*, London, 1984, p. 30.
6. Deut. 26: 5-9.

frequently underlined in certain psalms.[7] But in addition to looking back with awe and gratitude to Yahweh for this historic deliverance, the Israelites also had reason to look forward to the future in expectation of fuller and final deliverance under such figures as the prophet like Moses (Deut. 18: 15 18); the Messianic King who would sit on David's throne (II Samuel 7: 12–16), the Son of Man (Dan. 7), Elijah the Prophet (Mal. 4:5–6), the *ebed Yahweh* (Is. 42:1-9; 49:1-6 *etc*.) or even Yahweh himself who would appear on a certain great and notable day for judgement and salvation (Amos 5:18-20; Joel 1:15; 2:1,11; Zeph. 1:1,14, Zech. 14: 1).

Though these different concepts were employed in Israel in picturing this future hope, they were all linked somewhat because of their association with the Kingdom of God. Even during the best of times in Israel's history, conditions were by no means entirely satisfactory. At no time was the entire promised land 'from the wilderness and this Lebanon, as far as the great river, the river Euphrates, all the land of the Hittites to the Great Sea toward the going down of the Sun. . . .' (Josh. 1:4) even under the control of Israel. At no time did righteousness and justice cover the entire land as expected. The *berit* which Yahweh had made with Israel was being grossly violated. It is in this context that we may place Jeremiah's prophecy about the new Covenant (Jeremiah 31: 31-34). The covenant would be made in an unspecified future: 'Behold the days are coming. . . .' We may also note the expression 'after those days'. It would also be an effective covenant of righteousness: 'I will put my law within them...I will forgive their iniquity and I will remember their sin no more'. Time as a three dimensional phenomenon consisting of the past, the present and the future in Israel's religious experience is clearly discernible from what has been said thus far. This leads us to emphasize that a very important element in Israel's religion was the Messanic hope in its broadest sense. Israel's neighbours whose religions consisted of nature worship and who had a cyclic view of history had their future hopes based on the cycle of death and re-incarnation. As Oesterley and Robinson assure us they had no thought of a

---

7. *E.g.* Psalms 74: 12ff; 135:8–9; 136: 10–15.

distant future.[8] Thus Old Testament Messianism and eschatology had no real counterpart in the ancient Near East. The specifically Israelite projection toward the final goal of history was vividly lacking.[9] As Jakob Obersteiner has pointed out, the monarchy and the expectations it engendered and the proclamation and experience of judgement might have sharpened the hope of a Messiah in Israel, but it is doubtful whether these factors above can account for the genesis of this hope: 'Israel's own unique presentation of her God, and her faith in Yahweh's readiness to help her may have stimulated and developed messianic hope as we find it in the Bible, but they cannot have provided its origin. In the final analysis it goes back to divine revelation'.[10]

The position held here is that it is only within the confines of revealed and redemptive religion, as in Judaeo-Christian tradition, that we may find genuine messianic expectation. It is not surprising therefore that the nature religions of ancient Egypt, Babylon and other ancient Near Eastern cultures could not develop any messianic hope.

In the New Testament we are immediately confronted with the message that messianic expectation was already being fulfilled. According to Matthew's special source, John the Baptist sounded this note of fulfilment and summoned his hearers to eschatological decision: 'Repent for the kingdom of heaven is at hand'. He also spoke of a Coming One who would baptize his hearers with the Holy Spirit and with fire (Matthew 3:2, 11). For John the Baptist, the era of eschatological fulfilment was right at the door. This message re-echoes on the lips of Jesus (Matthew 4:17). Mark puts it very vividly: 'The time is fulfilled and the Kingdom of God is at hand(*engiken*); repent and believe the gospel' (1:15).

The difficulty in translating *engizein* has often been realized. It can mean 'to draw near', or 'to arrive', or 'to reach'.[11] C. H. Dodd with his doctrine of realised eschatology

---

8. W. D. E. Oesterley & T. H. Robinson, *Hebrew Religion: Its Origin and Development*, London, 1966, p. 375.

9. E. Jenni in *The Interpreter's Dictionary of The Bible*, vol 3, p. 361.

10. Jakob Obersteiner 'Messianism' in *Bauer's Encyclopaedia of Biblical Theology*, Vol. 2.

11. *Cf. e.g.* I. H. Marshall, *St Luke*, Exeter, p. 422.

had believed that the *word* implies that the Kingdom had fully arrived in the ministry of Jesus. He later modified his view in recognition of the fact that there would be a fuller manifestation of the Kingdom beyond history. In any case *engizein* can neither mean that the eschatological age has fully come, nor that it is entirely futuristic no matter how near it may be. The term implies from our own perspective that the Kingdom has been inaugurated through the incarnation, ministry, crucifixion and resurrection of Jesus; the present reality of the Kingdom is already being experienced through the forgiveness of sins, through signs and wonders (*semeia kai terata*), and through the gifts of the Holy Spirit, but the final consumation awaits the future.[12] The powers of the Age to Come have broken into the present evil age in the experience of believers, and the end of the latter age is now imminent. It is now the 'last hour' and 'the form of this world is passing away'.[13] Believers now live between the aeons in anticipation of the end of this Age and the final manifestation of the Messianic Era.

An important point to note in the New Testament is the emphasis on the once-for-all-ness, or unrepeatability of the eschatological and soteriological events of the incarnation, the crucifixion and the resurrection of Jesus Christ, at least by St Paul and the writer of Hebrews. 'Christ, having been offered *once* to bear the sins of many, will appear a second time, not to deal with sin but to save those who are eagerly waiting for him'.[14]

From all indications, therefore, Salvation-history in the New Testament as in the Old – in spite of the belief in the overlapping of the two Ages in the former is a meaningful and irreversible process with a beginning and an end, reaching out to a goal predetermined by God. This is far from the cyclic view of the dying and rising gods of the Graeco-Roman mystery religions. For Christians there is a past aspect of their *Heilsgeschichte* to which they look in retrospect; there is the present period of service and anticipation; and finally, there is the future kingdom whose consummation is being awaited.

12. S. E. Johnson, *The Gospel According to St Mark*, London, p. 43.
13. I Jn 2:18–19; I Cor. 7:31; see also Heb. 6: 4–5.
14. Heb. 9:28; *cf.* Rom. 6:9–10; Heb. 7:27; 9:12, 25–28.

This linear three-dimensional aspect of time is underlined in a concentrated form by Paul in relation to the Lord's Supper: 'For as often as you eat this bread and drink this cup, you proclaim the Lord's death until he comes' (I Cor. 11:26).

III Time, History and Eschatology According to Mbiti in Relation to the Akamba of Kenya.

Professor J. S. Mbiti is in no doubt a foremost African theologian and scholar of religion in our generation, and one cannot study religion or theology in Africa without referring to some of his many works. It was first of all in relation to the Akamba of Kenya that he put forward what he thought was the African conception of time and history.[15]

According to Mbiti, the question of time is of little or no academic interest to Africans. It is simply a composition of events which have occurred, or are taking place now, or are immediately to occur. What has not taken place or has no likelihood of immediate occurrence falls into the category of 'No-time'. But what is certain to occur or falls within the rhythm of natural phenomena is in the category of inevitable or potential time.[16] The most importance consequence of this, in his view, is that in African traditional understanding, time is a two-dimensional phenomenon with a long past, a present and virtually no future.

The linear concept of time in Western thought (as he saw it) with an indefinite past, a present and an infinite future is foreign to African thinking. For the African time moves 'backwards' and not 'forward', and people set their minds not on future things, but chiefly on what has taken place. To buttress his point, he undertakes a literary analysis of the Akamba verb which means 'to come'. He puts forward nine different tenses of this verb, and then claims that in the East African languages in which he had carried out his research, there were no concrete words to convey the idea of a distant future. The three verb tenses referring to the future cover the period of six months, or at most two years. As a result people

15. Mbiti's position is mainly expressed in two of his books: *African Religions and Philosophy*, 1969, pp. 15–28 and *New Testament Eschatology in an African Background*, especially pp. 24–61.
16. *African Religions and Philosophy*, pp. 15-17.

have little or no active interest in events that lie in the future beyond two years from any given time. Africans had no numerical or mathematical calenders and they expected the years to come and go in an endless rhythm. 'They expect the events of the rain season, planting, harvesting, dry season, rain season again, planting again, and so on to continue for ever'.[17]

Mbiti used the Swahili words *Sasa* and *Zamani* in his analysis in *African Religions and Philosophy*.[18] But in *New Testament Eschatology in an African Background* he employs the Kikamba: *Mituki* and *Tene*.[19] *Sasa* (or *Mituki*) covers the now period, having the sense of immediacy or nearness. *Zamani* (or *Tene*) on the other hand refers to the unlimited past. Whatever can be remembered belongs to the *Sasa* (*Mituki*) period. *Zamani* (*Tene*) overlaps with *Sasa* but generally it lies beyond memory: it is the distant incomprehensible past. Mbiti's claim is that the Akamba – and all Africans – can only think in terms of *Sasa* and *Zamani*, and never about the future.

For Mbiti, the African traditional concept of history runs along the same lines. History means backwards from the *Sasa* period to the *Zamani*, from the moment of intense experience to the period beyond which nothing can go:

> In traditional African thought, there is no concept of history moving 'forward' towards a future climax, or towards an end of the world. Since the future does not exist beyond a few months, the future can not be expected to usher in a golden age, or a radically different state of affairs from which is in the *Sasa* or *Zamani*. The notion of a Messianic hope or a final destruction of the world has no place in traditional concept of history. So African peoples have no belief in 'progress', the idea that the development of human activities and achievements move from lower to a higher degree. The people neither plan for the distant future nor build 'castles in the air'. The centre of gravity of human thought and activities is the *Zamani* period, towards which *Sasa* moves. People set their eyes on the *Zamani* since for them there is no 'world to come', such as is found in Judaism and Christianity'.[20]

17. *Ibid.*, p. 21.
18. pp. 22 ff.
19. pp. 27 ff.
20. *African Religions and Philosophy*, p. 23.

He acknowledges, however, the existence of a golden age in African perception but this age lies in the *Zamani* period, not in the very short or non-existent future. As far as he can see, only the Sonjo of Tanzania have any myths about the end of the world. His explanation is that, perhaps at one point in their history, their volcanic mountain erupted and caused 'an end of the world in their small country'. This event they have transformed to the unknown future, as a warning about possible future eruptions.[21] In any case, this belief by the Sonjo is not something that dominates their lives, and they go on living as if the idea did not exist.

But Mbiti thinks that in recent times, African perception of time and history is beginning to change. Because of Christian teaching, Western-type education and the invasion of modern technology African peoples are 'discovering' the future dimension of time. On the secular level this leads to national planning. In Church life, this 'discovery' creates a strong expectation of the millenium, and this makes Christians escape from the challenges of this life into the state of merely hoping and waiting for the life of paradise. Again, in his view, this strong millenial expectation often leads to the emergence of many small independent churches centred around individuals who symbolize, and more or less fulfil, this messianic expectation.[22]

IV An Evaluation

These views of Mbiti about the inability of the traditional African to grasp the future dimension of time have not gone unchallenged. One of the earliest critics of his views had been the late Byang Kato in his *Theological Pitfalls in Africa*.[23] Other critics include E. B. Kalibala, A. Lugira, and his (Mbiti's) former student Anatoli Tibaryehinda[24] The most recent criticism I have heard has been that of Professor O.

---

21. *Ibid.*, p. 24 with footnote
22. *Ibid.*, pp. 27–28, also *New Testament Eschatology in an African Background*, pp. 31–32.
23. Kisumu, Kenya: Evangel Publishing House, 1975, pp. 57–64.
24. *cf.* Kato, *ibid.*, for details. Anatoli's name is much longer than presented in the main body of this paper. The full name is Anatoli Tibaryehinda Balyesiima-Byaruhanga-Akiiki!

Onoge of the University of Jos, Nigeria in the 1987 Faculty of Arts Dean's lecture titled 'Afro-centric Thought: from Marcus Garvey to Amicor Cabral' at the University of Ife, Nigeria.

When Mbiti talks of time as being of little or no concern to Africans, he could not have been talking of time in the general sense but in the scientific sense – which seeks to place all happenings in the order in which they occurred, or at correctly proportioned intervals on a fixed scale. In that case Mbiti is talking of pre-literate Africans who could not read the arms of the clock or know the number of days in a particular calendar month. But they know that they have to set out on a long journey at cock-crow, they know when to clear the bush in anticipation of the early rains, *etc*. This dimension of illiteracy, Mbiti totally ignores. For him to claim that the traditional African can virtually not think or plan about the future is misleading and inconsistent. As he himself points out the Akamba people perform the Kuimithya initiation ceremony when a child is between five and fifteen years of age, and this is anticipated at birth. Again African parents ensure that their children find husbands and wives for the future in order to ensure that the family line is not extinguished.[25] In African societies there are prognosticators who seek to unravel mysteries pertaining to the future – including the distant future In Yoruba society, the diviner *babalawo* trains for a long period of time, from between ten to twelve years, during which time he commits a vast store of more than a thousand *odu*., *i.e.* oral traditions to help him in his divination, to memory. Is it conceivable for a trainee diviner not to anticipate the time he would qualify as a full-fledged practitioner in the future? How can people set their minds only on the *Zamani*, the distant past, because they do not believe in the world to come? In fact Africans believe in a good heaven of bliss and a bad heaven of potsherds and suffering. A good hereafter of bliss is assured for the African provided he is not a witch, and provided all the prescribed traditional rites have been performed by his children on earth. At least this is the belief. As a result African elders tell their children what to do when they die. This anticipated death is certainly not in the past but

25. See *African Religions and Philosophy*, p. 106.

in an undetermined future which could be more than ten years!

It is worth pointing out that indigenous empires – Benin, Oyo, Songhai, Ghana – existed in pre colonial Africa, and their rulers planned military campaigns, built walled and fortified cities, or dug trenches around their cities for years, a clear example being Benin. We have every reason to believe that the indigenous African, contrary to Mbiti's views, can think about the future no matter how imprecisely. As B. Kato put it: 'The Africans, including the Akamba people, may not have a clear understanding of the future, but that does not mean they cannot conceive of the future'.[26] An African grandmother who never went to school may not know the date of her birth, and she may not have a clear understanding of the future either; but the question is which people in the world through reasoning, even with the aid of statistical data, can claim to have a clear understanding of the future.

What the traditional African lacks is the belief in a messiah who would cause the end of the present world system, and usher in a new age. But again this deficiency is not peculiar to the African. Strictly speaking, it is only in biblical tradition that classical messianism exists. And it is an over-simplification for John S. Mbiti to say that the linear concept of history is 'Western'. It is only 'Western' in so far as this Judaeo-Christian concept has been popularized in Africa by European or American Missionaries. After all there are many people in the Western world who do not believe that there will ever be an end to the present world through divine intervention.

It is interesting to note that when Mbiti talks of Africans 'discovering' and 'extending' the future dimension of time, he does not give examples of Africans who still cling to the traditional religious system who now allow belief in the end of the world or in the coming of a Messiah to dominate their lives. He says this only of African Christians who are now influenced by the Bible. On the secular level he talks of African governments which plan for the future. Traditional African governments were not entirely bereft of future plans. What has now happened is that the plans of modern African

26. Kato, p. 61.

governments have become more scientific. But such governments do not necessarily (apart from individual believers in government, believe in the end of the world, or the coming of a Messiah as a result of the new discovery and exstension of the future dimension of time, and plan towards it.

V Conclusion

One may ask why J. S. Mbiti has propounded this peculiar theory of time and history and applied it to Africans. One may be able to see that he had, at least, two genuine Christian concerns in his *New Testament Eschatology in an African Background* .[27] The first was how to deal with the nagging problem of apocalyptic speculations and date-fixing for the parousia and the end of the world. He was worried that the type of eschatology presented by missionaries to Africans is exclusively 'futurist'. Secondly he was concerned about the indiscriminate proliferation of independent Christian sects. According to him, because of the so-called signs about the end of the world, some individual believers go as far as setting dates for the 'End'. But African apocalyptic speculators like their Montanist predecessors fall into the mistake of date-fixing not because they have just made an astonishing discovery about the future dimension of time, but because they have chosen to ignore the balanced biblical teaching which discourages such wild speculation (*e.g.* Mk 13:32; Acts 1:7; II Thess. 2:1ff). Nor can it be said that it is this sudden discovery that has caused the proliferation of sects in church history, or African church history specifically. There are other ways of tackling these problems of the church in Africa apart from Mbiti's theory which implies that African Christians should not be informed about the parousia or about the end of the world.

27. See pp. 51-55.

GOD'S RELATIONSHIP TO HISTORY IN PANNENBERG

Timothy Bradshaw

Introduction

The aim of this paper is to spell out Pannenberg's rejection of what he takes to be the current options on offer of models of God's relationship to history, and to give a critical account of his own proposals so that we might begin to identify problems and possible reforms for evangelical theology.

Pannenberg may be particularly useful as a catalyst in this area because he tries to take up the Biblical tradition, especially apocalyptic, and is committed to seek a new synthesis incorporating the claims of revelation and those of modernity. He also criticises both wings, liberal and conservative, and could be said to 'seek to go beyond their polar opposition while taking what is essential from each'. Whether or not one buys into his total system, and there are very good grounds for not doing so, his acute presuppositional criticism is a healthy stimulus for orthodox theology. He offers a keen challenge to return to scripture and reassess the received doctrine of the God of Jesus. Pannenberg is, in short, a breaker of moulds and we must be sure to take careful note of helpful fresh insights that may result from his determined restructuring.

The plan of the paper will be, firstly, to sketch out Pannenberg's critique of both orthodox and modernist understandings of God and the world; secondly, we will review his own proposed revision of the traditional framework including particularly Pannenberg's increasing trinitarian emphasis coming across very clearly in the untranslated volume of essays which hopefully will soon be published in English as *Basic Questions* volume 4;[1] thirdly, an appraisal will be offered, and finally areas of special importance for evangelical theology will be raised.

---

1. *Grundfagen systematischer Theologie*, Band 2, Gottingen, Vandenhoech und Ruprecht,1980 (hereafter referred to as 'GST2').

GOD'S RELATIONSHIP TO HISTORY IN PANNENBEG.

1. Problems Pannenberg perceives with positions ancient and modern

Fear of dualism lies at the heart of Pannenberg's rejection of both the conservative and the modernist doctrines of God and the world. He considers both schools to have put asunder God from non-divine reality, and his theological enterprise is largely taken up with making a fresh synthesis of the two. Tillich says that the dynamo of the history of theology has been wrestling with the question of how to unite 'the principle of identity and the principle of detachment'.[2] How does he conduct his critique?

Against the modernist line of theology Pannenberg anticipated the kinds of critique of the enlightenment recently made in Britain by Keith Ward and Colin Gunton. Pannenberg attacks the anthropocentric orientation of liberal and existentialist theologies, which make man the measure of all reality. Modern man has become self obsessed. He now fails to see that he is dependent upon the context in which he finds himself for both his being and his knowing. The legacy of the enlightenment and of Kant has left theology in the grip of a metaphysic of subjectivism and positivism. Man has alienated himself from his history and has sought to gain his meaning from within himself.

Pannenberg severely attacks the existentialising version of anthropocentric theology for dehistoricising the faith. The content of Israel's salvation history, culminating with Jesus and the church, is lost by being funnelled into the individual's personal sense, oscillating between alienation authenticity, of the present moment. 'Historicity' has become narrowed solipsistically into the individual's immediate experience. Pannenberg says that

> Heidegger's concept of the experience of anxiety and being-unto-death achieves something analogous to the historical relativisation of world historical content: the liberation of man to his real historicity in existential freedom.[3]

---

2. *Perspectives on Nineteenth and Twentieth Century Protestant Theology.* Braaten, Carl E. (ed) London, p. 75.
3. *Basic Questions in Theology*, trans. George H. Kem, London, 1970, p. 234 (hereafter referred to as 'BQ1').

Pannenberg rejects this identification of historicity as personal authenticity because in effect it displaces not only the reality of history but also the God of that history. Such theology abandons its objectivity both in terms of man's world and in terms of the Lord of that world.

> The emancipation of historicity from history, the reversal of the relationship between the two so that history is grounded in the historicity of man – this seems to be the end of the way which began when modern man made man instead of God the one who bears history.[4]

Against the Kantian divide between reason and faith, man and God, history and revelation, Pannenberg seeks to harmonise and synthesise, to locate man in his milieu of historical reality and meaning where he finds meaning and context.

The interpretation of Jesus by Wilhelm Herrmann and by Schleiermacher, for example, is wholly wrong in that they seek the revelation of God in the isolated person of Jesus,[5] cutting Jesus off from his historical tradition and context, the history of Israel. Likewise modernist christology cuts Jesus off from his God: 'Jesus of Nazareth without his message about the Father and His coming kingdom is not conceivable . . . the man Jesus is not accessible without his God'.[6] Jesus must be interpreted in his historical and, inseparably, his theological context.

Pannenberg's version of historicism rebuts the modern world view which fits a naturalistic, positivistic grid over history. Modern theology encrusts itself with the doctrine that historical events are always identical in nature and Pannenberg protests: 'The levelling of historical particularity, brought about by one-sided emphasis in the typical and analogous, threatens to elevate the postulate of the homogeneity of all events to the status of a principle'.[7] He continues:

> Theology must take a burning interest in this side of historical work. It is characteristic of the activity of the transcendent God,

4. BQ1 35.
5. BQ1 67.
6. 'Christologie und Theologie', GST2 p. 130.
7. BQ1 47.

whose essence is not adequately expressed in any cosmic order but remains free from every such order, that it constantly gives rise to something new in reality, something never before present. For this reason theology is interested primarily in the individual, particular and contingent.[8]

Joyce Baldwin in the introduction to her Tyndale commentary on Daniel welcomes Pannenberg's new framework in that it breaks with the old grid of rationalism and reductivism which has for so long rendered the insights of Biblical apocalyptic nugatory.[9]

Pannenberg therefore castigates modernist types of theology for their subjectivity and failure to accept historical objective content, and for their narrow positivistic exclusion of the unheard of event in history which effectively divorces God from the process. Autonomous, empiricist man has become the measure of everything. God is either a function of human interior sensibilities or is too far distanced to be of relevance.

Pannenberg matches his critique of modernism with his rejection of the orthodox Christian tradition of the triune God creating the world, revealing himself to it and redeeming it. The criticism is essentially the same as he turned against the liberal tradition: conservative theology also divorces history from God. Pannenberg thinks that conservative doctrine is theologically, as well as philosophically, untenable because its idea of God is too external and too dualistic: for Pannenberg God is *all-determining reality,* emphasising the 'all'. Both in terms of epistemology and ontology the conservative position fails to do justice to this truth about God, according to Pannenberg.

In *Revelation as History,* Pannenberg rejected the conservative view of Biblical revelation and the inspiration of Scripture on the grounds that these doctrines rest on *a priori* decisions of faith and fail to account of ordinary secular historical critical study. He says that this procedure is akin to a dualistic gnosticism claiming authority for a purely private body of knowledge, a body of knowledge which is insulated from the canons of ordinary common sense scrutiny. This

8.   BQ1 48.
9.   Daniel, 1978, IVP, p.16.

kind of theology makes authoritarian claims and refuses to justify them.[10] Barth's version of Word-based theology comes in for equally severe criticism as an exercise in ghetto theology.

Conservative theology splits the field of knowledge into the sacred and the secular and thus is guilty of dualism of knowing. This, for Pannenberg, is not only faulty philosophically, but offends theologically the understanding of God as the all-determining reality. If God is the one behind all truth and being then how can theology operate with this kind dualism of knowledge? The secular area of thought is not to be so sharply ruled off as irrelevant for our thinking about God. Pannenberg therefore cannot accept the understanding of salvation history as entirely different from secular history, nor can there be any special inspiration not available in principle in the whole field of human thought.

Pannenberg likewise applies his complaint to the area of Christology. The traditional trinitarianism of the conservative theology results in the person of Christ being insufficiently integrated into the course of ordinary human history. In his article 'The God of History' Pannenberg sums up his rejection of classical trinitarianism: 'The God of the classical doctrine of the Trinity is still only secondarily the God of history and of historical revelation'.[11] The traditional trinitarian dogma has burdened theology with having to uphold an absurd and meaningless relationship between God and the world; a changeless God with a contingent historical process into which the divine Son has somehow to fit.

In short, Pannenberg rejects both left and right, accusing each side of deistic dualism, of excluding the all-determining reality from the history of mankind, of forms of authoritarian abstract dogmatism. What is his proposed way forward? It must be one which will do justice to the whole of human experience and to the real events of history.

10. *Revelation as History,* trans. D. Granskou, New York, 1968; London, 1969, chapter 1.
11. GST2 123.

2. Pannenberg's revision of traditional theism

Pannenberg sees no way forward in either the traditionalist or the radical proposals on their own. He wishes to take up their valid points and to reject their errors. Again it is strongly arguable that he is very concerned that what he considers to be a proper Christian doctrine of God be given a controlling role in his new proposals. God is the determining reality over the whole of human existence without exception, and this means that the division of sacred versus secular is not an ultimate one, or even a valid one. It is probably true to say that this central concern for synthesis, for the integrated unity of the whole of reality lies behind his theological programme. This is amply borne out in his understanding of revelation and the historical character of our knowledge of God to which we first turn.

A. Revelation and history

Pannenberg is of great interest to the evangelical because he insists on the need for God to reveal himself if we are to have any knowledge of God. Barth, he says, is correct in upholding the dictum: 'by God alone can God be known', and Pannenberg points out that this originated with Hegel. God is not God if we can somehow subject him to purely human rational inspection and discovery. Knowledge of God must be given by God. On the other hand we live in the modern scientific, critical world and we cannot escape the responsibility of using all the modern critical apparatus on the material on which we base our faith. Pannenberg himself asks:

> Is there a way out of this dilemma? Obviously there is a way only if the claim of Christian proclamation to derive from an experience of God does not remain a mere assertion but is capable of verification.[12]

Pannenberg wants to open the claim of the gospel to the scrutiny of every possible modern critical discipline, but he goes on:

> This need not involve a court of appeal prior to the Biblical revelation of God before which the latter would have to legitimate itself. Such a

12. BQ2 206-7.

court of appeal would be incompatible with the majesty of divine revelation. Christian speech about God can be verified only in such a way that it is the revelation of God itself which discloses that about man and his world in relation to which its truth is proved.[13]

Critical verification then, for Pannenberg, is itself a product of divine revelational activity. The way he sets about achieving this synthesis between revelation and critical reason is, of course, by his programme of revelation as history. The whole course of history, history taken as a whole without any *a priori* selection of a specially inspired strand, argues Pannenberg, indirectly reveals God. He sketches out his doctrine of indirect self revelation, taking on Barth's definition of revelation and stretching it out across the whole canvas of time. God reveals himself, but in the whole of history whose meaning will be clear at the end of time. Jesus' life, death and resurrection all read by critical historical method, taken against the background of the apocalyptic thought world of the day for which the resurrection of the dead is the revelatory end time event – this whole nexus of event and meaning discloses to the historian that Jesus is the end time event in advance, proleptically.

For Pannenberg revelation involves not only the activity of God but the being of God; again Barth's influence is strong, but this revelation is appropriated indirectly, that is, through the medium of our reasoning and interpreting minds rather than in an experience of unquestionable power which compels acceptance and quashes all careful consideration and reflection. The self-revelation of God is going on as history proceeds, but in the history of Jesus we have a point of focus, a point where this is disclosed to our normal historical reason and therefore indirectly. History throws up many glimmers of the divine, hints and intimations of immorality and of the mysterious power behind things. But in Christs resurrection we gain a clear advance picture of revelation, of God's self-disclosure.

This is Pannenberg's answer to the need to reunite revelation and history, the sacred with the secular, faith with critical modern reason. In effect he abolishes the distinction. David McKenzie correctly observes that Pannenberg does

13. *Ibid.*

away with supernatural knowledge while insisting on divine initiative, on revelation, for any knowledge of God, McKenzie asks:

> But how is it possible for faith to be based only on the revelation of God if there is no supernatural knowledge? I believe that the answer to this question can serve as a key to understanding Pannenberg's approach in general. I submit that Pannenberg wants to link natural knowledge and revelation.[14]

Revelation compels itself onto the properly analytical historically enquiring mind because for Pannenberg the evidence for the resurrection of Jesus commands assent and therefore the Christian understanding of how things are becomes inevitable. Historical reason and revelation have been so defined as to make them inseparable. But just as Pannenberg can affirm the rationality of revelation in Jesus and his resurrection, so he also says and for the same reasons that this is provisional because the evidence may change and some new factor may arise which compels a reversal of the positive view of the resurrection. It is worth noting that this is the precise reverse of Bultmann's position which is that mere historical evidence is irrelevant for matters of faith.

By this Christological focus Pannenberg suggests that he has managed to do justice to the revelational aspect and to the critical rationality aspect of the theological problem. He was quoted above as saying that ' Christian speech about God can be verified only in such a way that it is the revelation of God itself which discloses that about man and his world in relation to which its truth is proved' The Jesus revelation discloses the proleptic nature of all reality and all reason, both of which are historical and emerge from the open future towards which they in turn move. The Jesus revelation is a disclosure as to how things are generally, it is a window into what we otherwise only glimpse.

Pannenberg synthesises reason and revelation by means of an historicist view of the world heavily indebted to Hegel. History is hermeneutically bringing meaning into being and human minds, which are not distinct from this web, thematise

14. *Wolfhart Pannenberg and Religious Philosophy,* Washington DC, p. 14.

or formulate the significance inherent in the developing process. Our reason sketches and reflects the ongoing meaning of history. Hence faith and reason share the same kind of structure of anticipating the shape of the whole and trusting what they take to be the central controlling principle behind things. Not only does the revelation of Jesus and his resurrection disclose the shape of reality as a hermeneutical process which is future orientated, it also discloses that this is a trinitarian metaphysic, and to this we now turn.

B. Trinitarian immanentism

It would be a mistake to give the impression that we can make a fundamental distinction in Pannenberg's theology between the order of knowing and the order of being because his synthesising tendency operates to meld them together in the hermeneutical history which constitutes the whole, but we now look at the nature of the relationship of God to the world already implicit in his view of revelation.

In the first volume of *Basic Questions in Theology* Pannenberg wrote

> the God who constitutes history has himself fully entered the process of history in his revelation. But he has done so in such a way that precisely as he is transmitted in a process of tradition, he is at the same time the future of this history, the coming God who . . . is always distinguishing himself in a new way from what happens in this history.[15]

This is simply another way of stating the doctrine of revelation as history, bearing in mind the identification of God and revelation. Pannenberg has produced a model of God and the world which revises the upstairs-downstairs, supernatural model; in favour of what seems initially to be a flat temporal model with the open future as the free source of the line of the developing finite history made up of the present and past.

For Pannenberg everything is encompassed by the category of history and the temporal, with God as the open, free future releasing events into finite history, although 'finite' is not a very good term to employ in Pannenberg's case. But God' as we have just read, indwells history's present and past as well

15. BQ1, 158.

as being its future. The whole finished story of history will constitute God's very being as revealed' indirect form. This is a trinitarian metaphysic, according to Pannenberg: the future, present and past correspond to the Father, Spirit and Son.

The Spirit is the divine capacity for events to go beyond themselves, to transcend themselves and to develop by incorporating new events or insights as they arrive from the future. The Spirit enables the present to take the past forward into the novelty bestowed by the future which can never fully be predicted. God is immanent in this process of historical advance and self-transcendence and is at the same time hovering before the process as its future.

The Son is no pre-existent being subsequently incarnated in Jesus. Rather Jesus was constituted the Son by the event of the resurrection retroactively and not just retrospectively. The process of history itself therefore contributes towards the identity of the Godhead. The Sonship of Jesus illustrates how, for Pannenberg, all being has its true meaning, and therefore its being, ahead of it and ultimately in the eschaton. This he sees as the relevance of apocalyptic thought which saw that the puzzling events of history would become clear at the end time.

Pannenberg regards his doctrine as a revision of Hegel's ontology which only failed because it absolutised the philosopher's own era and absolutised the power of God at the expense of his freedom. Pannenberg feels that his future reorientation of history and his emphasis on the divine freedom from the future enables him to keep what he regards as the advantages of the Hegelian metaphysic without its drawbacks.

It is important to stress that he rejects firmly the view of process theology[16] according to which God actually is at risk in the course of historical events: his sovereignty is sacrificed to enhance his immanent sensitivity and vulnerability to the world's free activity. Pannenberg in his essay, 'The God of History', says that Process theology 'loses the absoluteness of God by making him a factor in the universe alongside others and in interaction with them'.[17] Pannenberg indeed

16 *der Gott der Geschichte,* GST2 118
17. GST2 118.

goes to great lengths to distance himself from this surrender of divine Lordship into the soup of the finite. God's freedom over against the historical process is, for Pannenberg, secured by his futurity. That is why we may not even accurately say that God 'exists': he does not exist as an item in the universe as do all the other items known by us. God, says Pannenberg using Heidegger's distinction, is not *vorhanden*, not 'on hand' like an article in a shop. This is the same point that Macquarrie makes in his distinction between beings and Being:[18] the latter transcends the former while bestowing their existence on them; it is more a dynamic version of Tillich's 'ground of being' definition of God.

Pannenberg then steers between orthodox external and unchanging deity, over-influenced by Greek thought and not Biblical enough, and Process ideas of a vulnerable God at the mercy of history and really changed by it and in it. Hegel and the trinitarian doctrine offer Pannenberg his way of forging what he takes to be a new kind of synthesis doing justice to divine majesty and to real divine involvement in history whereby the divine being is really affected. It is after all only Biblical to think of God and the history of his activity as inseparable. God must not be thought of confined by the world, says Pannenberg, but as completing it through himself.

This is precisely what did happen in the case of the Sonship of Jesus. Pannenberg has abolished a preexisting, already completed trinitarian life of God independent of any creation. God's being and historical activity are not to be separated. Pannenberg says that 'the resurrection of Jesus is...just as constitutive for the Godhead of the Father as it is for the sonship of Jesus. Without Jesus' resurrection the Father proclaimed by Jesus would not be God. That means that the history of the Son concerns the divinity of the Father himself'.[19] This accounts for the fact that God's very existence is debated and controversial and always will be till the eschaton: the order of being is reflected in the order of knowing. Pannenberg concludes his article The God of History from which we have been quoting with this

18. *Principles of Christian Theology.*
19. *'der Gott der Geschichte',* GST 123.

unequivocal statement of real internal relations of God with history:

> Both the fact that the divinity of God is still at stake and the fact that God's future reality is already at work in the process of history, both these facts can be expressed by the doctrine of the Trinity through the tension between the creative activity of the Father and his dependence upon the work of the Son and the Spirit for the realisation of the Kingdom of God'.[20]

Pannenberg's position then is that God, whose preexistent being cannot be called fully trinitarian, freely determines himself to be determined as he invests himself into the process of history and is genuinely affected by it. But God is the one who sends history from the freedom of the future, leading us to a dialectic: God's being and identity are affected decisively by the course of history and yet God is the one deciding the course of history from the future. The dialectic is our only answer to the issue of Jesus' sonship: he was constituted Son by the resurrection and this means that he always was so – Pannenberg leaves us to oscillate to and fro. This dialectic is crowned when we ask of the existence of the essential Trinity: does the Trinity depend on creation or has it an essential life in and of itself? Pannenberg answers that God did not have to create the world, but given that he did then he is so linked to it that his eternal essence depends upon the outcome of its history.

3. A Brief appraisal of Pannenberg's doctrine
Pannenberg has fashioned a subtle view in which the world is invested with the very being of God so that God is himself constituted in and through historical events, a radical panentheism. But God also remains the Lord over the process from the future, and here is the special and perhaps saving twist.

This is a Hegelian doctrine of quite a pure strain: the deity expresses itself as the totality of the process of history which grows or evolves by taking up the past into the future as the spirit of history continually reconstitutes both thought and reality in ever new syntheses of meaning. It may be unfair on

20. *Ibid.*, p 127.

Pannenberg to say that his Son is really a pictorial way of presenting the truth of the whole: after all, what exactly is revealed apart from the union in distinction of the Son and Father in the Spirit, distinctions which rest on temporal differences? God invests his essence, or even gives his essence of pure freedom a finite form. The whole of history is revelation and revelation involves divine essence. Has God revealed himself to himself through the medium of the whole process of the historical consciousness of humanity?

I have no doubt that McKenzie is wrong in denying that Pannenberg's metaphysic is one of Hegelian real relations, and also that he is wrong in locating Pannenberg in the process theology school, because Pannenberg seeks to protect the freedom of God as well as divine immanence.[21] We must place Pannenberg in the more subtle category of idealism. God is the beyond in the midst of the process, whose truth is disclosed in the unfolding of the event of the Son, the particular exemplification of the universal. The spirit breathes through the whole, drawing all thought and reality towards each other and towards the final point of ultimate unification, the eschaton. Macquarrie calls the spirit 'unitive being', and the title also fits for Pannenberg's pneumatology.

The model we are left with is in fact more subtle than a linear one. It is more truly Hegelian. All truth and all events are not simply adding to their precursors: they are taken forward into ever new configurations of meaning until the end time when all is taken into the one final reality. Everything finds its true identity only at the ultimate eschaton, since until then meaning is always changing, even according to Pannenberg, after an individual's death. This is a radically objectivistic system and has pared away the standing or ontological status of the individual subject, which becomes in effect a moment taken up and then reconstituted into the flow of time. The being of each individual is decided by its meaning, a decision lying outside the subjective will of that individual after death.

It is hard to see how Pannenberg can escape the logical conclusion of the reabsorption of the historical into the deity at the end of time. All things and all thought are moving towards

21. *Op cit*, p. 129.

the point of unity, the point of the final futurity of the free God, the point at which the final meaning of all will be located. Then God will have realised his own identity as triune and this is the obverse of the whole of history finding its final meaning. This is exactly the logic of revelation as history: Pannenberg has identified the divine and the historical and has left only a dialectireal assertion to distinguish them. The historical process is at best the body or form assumed by the freely ordaining deity. God is as to the world as a mind, or better a free personality, is to the body: that seems to me to be the logical completion of this system. When the future is no longer the future to the now completed corpus of temporality, what then differentiates the divine from the finite?

Until that final end time event indeed Pannenberg has really been relying on the Hegelian dialectic of union and differentiation to prevent a straight identification of the immanent spirit with finite reality. This union and distinction is the trinitarian structure of things, a structure derived from temporal distinction of past and future being knit together in the present. God the spirit continually enlivens the body of history and indeed is the reason why there is freedom in history at all, a point of great apologetic potential. But Pannenberg can tell us that

> The element of transcendence in spirit suggests that after all it might be neither wise nor necessary to admit a fundamental distinction between a human spirit and a divine spirit...the creature participates in the spirit and I ventureto say in the divine spirit by by transcendence itself... thus the idea of spirit allows us to do justice to the transcendence of God and at the same time to explain his immanence in creation. Theology loses this chance when a fundamental distinction is accepted between a divine and human spirit .[22]

God is not a factor in the world as Process theology indicates. Rather for Pannenberg God is the dynamic life suffusing the whole while being beyond the sum of the totality of all historical events, in the same way that life is not just the sum total of the parts of the body: life is in each tiny part of the body, unites these parts, lives in the whole

---

22. *Spirit, Faith and Church*, by Pannenberg, Dulles and Braaten, Philadelphia, 1970, p. 19.

organism and yet is not confined to them. On the other hand life is not conceivable without the form of the body. Freedom needs the richness of form, but is not derivable from form. This is idealist metaphysics with all its synthesising fascination. Freedom invests itself into form, constantly uniting itself with and differentiating itself from that form, returning through this path of dialectical union and distinction, perhaps like the boomerang returning in its flight, back to itself enriched by this historical process. A divine kenosis returns through the historical process to plerosis. An undefined freedom puts itself forth and discovers its true trinitarian form and identity.

Pannenberg offers us this revision of an idealist historicism with its many insights and many problems: What can we learn from this work?

4. Areas of importance for Evangelical Theology

A. Revelation and History

Pannenberg cuts against evangelical theology by his refusal to acknowledge the authority of the canon of Scripture as special revelation in and of itself and for the same reason he declines to recognise that special illumination by the Spirit is needed for understanding and appropriating the truth of God. Pannenberg insists on a single field of knowledge and unaided rationality. For Panneberg the spirit is universally already involved prompting fresh projections or horizons of meaning; even our acknowledgement of Jesus as the Son is achieved by way of general historical hermeneutic.

This procedure is the very reverse of Barth's ruling out of natural theology: Pannenberg rules out the inbreaking of the Word and Spirit in favour of an unbroken epistemological continuum of spirit-breathed hermeneutic in which all mankind lives and moves and has its being. Pannenberg has immense confidence in human interpretive rationality. Unlike Aquinas he thinks that proper hermeneutical reasoning can deliver the understanding of the trinitarian nature of God. For Pannenberg reason, if accurately used, has the capacity to reach into heaven, itself – because heaven itself is already inside the ongoing process of the history of human thought, because God is the all-determining reality. Unlike classical natural theology Pannenberg does not believe that grace and revelation complete nature and rational investigation, rather they are two sides of the one coin. If anything Pannenberg is less Augustinian and Pauline than Aquinas in taking seriously the factor of sin in the potentiality of human thought to reach God.

My own conclusion here is that we cannot escape making some deep distinction between the book of nature and that of grace and that Pannenberg's synthesis is purchased at too high a price in abolishing this distinction. Grace must break into our unaided minds to enable us to know God and to think clearly about him. Notwithstanding that Pannenberg can reply that in his system God is always breaking into the present, a different kind of influence is required from that in the universal field of knowing, a moral and spiritual regenerative act of grace is needed from outside of the historical continuum. Romans 1 compels some such conclusion.

Although I feel bound to make the distinction between secular and sacred knowing and cannot go along with a radical synthesis of the two in idealist fashion, yet I do think that the idealist tradition and Pannenberg's use of it has lessons for our consideration of reason and faith. Pannenberg is not a foundationalist: for him we are already in the sea of faith which is also the sea of reason. For the evangelical once we are in Christ and the sphere of his revelation, then I think we can also say that reason is primarily interpretative and hermeneutical, elucidating the content of revelation in terms of contemporary thought – rather than pretending to have some isolated separate standpoint from which we criticise that revelation on which we depend. Henry Vander Groot likens the process to pervading influence experienced by the reader of say a Sartre novel

Though the Bible's vision of the world is authoritative and thus confronts its reader with a demand rather than an option, *how* the Bible subjects its reader is similar to how the sympathetic reader of a Sartre novel becomes taken in. . . . As he is thus overpowered by the world of the Bible – which often forms a sharp contrast to the world to which he has become accustomed – he is transformed; his mind is renewed, his sensibilities are deepened and hallowed.

The strange world of the Bible becomes his and he now goes about trying to make the world of his life relevant to the new world that he has discovered and that has compelled him to accept it at the deepest level of existence. It is in this way that man is transformed and controlled by the word of God. The revelation of the word of God becomes his context.[23]

Biblical revelation has a rich tapestry of cognitive, interpretable, objective content, and this is a point made by Pannenberg against modern reductivists, and we should as it were make that our own environment of mental life. The content of Biblical revelation is in fact far richer than Pannenberg's rather narrow apocalypticism would suggest and our reason needs to appropriate the richness of this content. Ongoing developments in secular thought will of course feed into this appropriation and elucidation.

Pannenberg's combination of rational defence of the resurrection along with his adherence to its historical provisionality demands a response from evangelical theology which claims to ground itself on the saving acts of God in history. Pannenberg posits the distinction between the logical possibility of evidence arising to destroy faith in the resurrection and psychological certainty in the believer. This is surely preferable to existentialising denials of the relevance of historical happenedness: Pannenberg insists on the need for a real concrete event to have occurred. This raises a most interesting question as to what we mean by an historical event. To say that something is historical means first that it actually happened. But secondly it usually implies that not only did it happen but that we know it happened because of accessible historical data. Pannenberg certainly affirms the resurrection as a result of his critical analysis of the available evidence. He would deny it as an event on the basis of a kerygmatic faith acceptance. The act of creation is historical in that it happened, but not in that we know it on the basis of purely historical data. We know it happened because we are given the inside information that it did. Evangelical theology could prefer this line and rests its certainty on the fact that the inside story is given in the text rather than on a purely secular historical analysis. But, unless it is to adopt the Barthian dualism, it must be prepared to be wise after the event and to

23. *Interpreting the Bible in Theology and the Church,* Lewiston , New York, 1984, p. 42.

spell out the connections of the event with secular historical questioning, even if it has to use the pending tray when the answers are not always perfectly clear.

Pannenberg again adds spice to this theological meal by his rejection of a third possible understanding of the term historical: that is that any event, to be historical, must be totally analogous to all other events, that a wholly different event is out of the question. For Pannenberg the novel is part of history and therefore we cannot rationally exclude the claims of any event *a priori*. He picks out the modern assumption that historical tends to imply a naturalistic world view. Clearly his argumentation here is very helpful to the case of orthodox Christianity.

B. God and the World

Finally let us ask how Pannenberg can help us clarify our understanding of God's relationship with the world. Keith Ward, in his *Rational Theology and the Creativity of God*, gives this opinion:

> By a rejection of the basic doctrine of self sufficiency one can move to the idea of a truly creative being, which can freely choose to bring about subjects of awareness other than himself, and thereby actualise new forms of value which would not otherwise exist.[24]

Ward says that Christian theology has failed to articulate her revelation of a truly creative God who is affected by the creation, and is not as external as traditional theology has asserted. 'If genuinely free creatures are admitted, there is an overwhelming argument against divine immutability and for divine temporality. . . . The creation is consequent upon God's knowledge, which depends in turn upon free creaturely acts; so God must be conceived as responding to free acts moment by moment, as they are decided. This means that we have to 'conceive Divine creation as a gradual and temporal process, depending partly on possibilities in his own being and partly on creatures. In a strictly limited sense, God can be changed from without'.[25] Although this was written after Pannenberg's articles appeared, it expressed the problem

24. *Rational Theology and the Creativity of God*, Oxford, 1982, p. 87.
25. *Ibid.*, p. 151-2.

Pannenberg addresses. Pannenberg maintains that the Biblical God is no immutable deity but relates to history in a real way, that is his being and identity are bound to the outcome of the course of history. At the same time God controls what happens in history from the open future, but the point is that Pannenberg has devised a way of formulating a doctrine of God in which God is affected by world events. Let us note that Pannenberg does not suggest that God's futurity can change, and that therefore provided that the case for theism holds up God would not be, for example, the God of the fixed past. Pannenberg in other words does not seem to presuppose aspects of deity which are not subject to change.

Perhaps the central teaching to consider is Pannenberg's idea of divine self-determination to be affected by the world. Given a more orthodox framework which does not define creaturely reality as the epiphenomen of spirit, is this a helpful suggestion for our doctrine of God? The God of Abraham is not thereby in any sense susceptible to changes in his character, but he has decided to bring into existence free wills which are intended to live in covenant with him. The Lord's prayer, for instance, seems to me to imply that God sees himself in some such way: we are told to pray that God's will be done, an extraordinary command which implies that the prayers of the faithful do have an impact on, and are desired to have an impact on, how the Lord of history rules events.

But God must be complete and wholly stable in his identity, not *en route* to it, to be the Biblical Lord of history to whom we can confidently address our prayers. Pannenberg knows this hence his stress on freedom and futurity, but his historicised trinitarianism subjects God to too much change. Christian faith knows that there is a God above temporality, external to the one continuum of past, present and future, because God breaks into time to redeem it. History itself, as Reinhold Niebuhr pithily put it, is not messianic or redemptive,[26] not even, we may add, from its future.

A better model for divine immanence in creation focuses on the act of God rather than his essence, even when that essence is defined as freedom. God is present in creation in a way more akin to an artist's presence in the work of art than to the

26. *Faith and History,* London, 1949, preface, p.v.

immanence of our life in our body. By running these types of model together. Pannenberg makes history too divine and God too historical. But he challenges us to better in revised models.

HISTORY, CRITICISM AND BIBLICAL THEOLOGY

J. Gordon McConville

History or Theology?

The aim of the present paper is to ask how biblical theology has responded, and may respond, to the challenge posed by the rise of biblical criticism. More precisely, we shall ask how theological statements may be made on the basis of the Bible, once it has been recognized and accepted that the Bible is susceptible of historical investigation. The term biblical theology is meant in a general sense, referring to the synthetic theological task that follows, or perhaps accompanies, the analytical tasks of historical inquiry and exegesis. The scope of the study is confessing scholarship widely understood. We shall be concerned in the end, however, with the question whether the issues raised are more acute, or just different, for evangelical theology, and in what ways evangelical theology does and can make a distinctive contribution to the wider debate.

It hardly needs saying, therefore, that we are taking for our subject one of the great problematical issues of 20th century theology. It would not be going too far to say that all the theological movements of the century have been in some way attempts to appropriate for the modern church, or modern humanity, the events and ideas found and witnessed to in the Bible. It follows that it will be almost impossible to do justice to the subject in the course of one paper! I propose to try to show however, that there are certain recurring and underlying dimensions of the question of history and theology by tracing a line through some representative figures and works from the so-called 'History of Religions' school to the present.

The questions put by history to theology in the 19th century are expressed sharply by William Wrede (a member of the 'History of Religions' school, which also, incidentally, included Troeltsch) in an essay entitled *The Task and Methods of 'New Testament Theology'*.[1]

---

1. First published in 1897; translated by Robert Morgan in *idem, The Nature of New Testament Theology*, London, 1973, pp. 68–116.

At the centre of the essay stands the claim: 'the church rests on history, but historical reality cannot escape investigation and this investigation of historical reality has its own laws.'[2] In his pursuit of this somewhat spiked axiom, it has to be said that Wrede established certain principles of historical study from which few today, in the age of hermeneutics, would dissent. He, for his part, was writing at a time when the historical consciousness to which the Enlightenment had given impetus was percolating only haphazardly into the explicitly confessional attempts to do biblical theology. His *bête noire* was the kind of theology which took inherited categories and read them out of the biblical text whether they were there or not. This kind of concern is in our day a commonplace, but we owe the fact in part to Wrede's insistence that all biblical discourse was produced in response to and in the context of particular circumstances and needs; it is not a compendium of answers to the reader's questions, in which every phrase may be squeezed for theological capital.[3] Wrede had a particular view, however, of the nature of the historical task. His contention was that the business of NT Theology was essentially to describe a set of historical religious phenomena, the evidence for which was contained in the New Testament *and* in other contemporary literature. For Wrede, the demise of the doctrine of the inspiration of the Scripture meant that the canon, or any idea of such, could no longer occupy any special place in the study which he nevertheless continued to call New Testament Theology. This was because he believed the proper object of study was the religious convictions and movements which lay behind the literature rather than the literature as such. With inspiration gone, there could be nothing normative about any particular set of documents. What dogmatics did with the results of historical investigation was its own affair.

Wrede thus not only issues a call to an autonomous historical research, but also poses sharply the question about its relationship with theology. Wrede's understanding of it was relatively simple: without inspiration there was no canon;

2. *Ibid.*, p.73.
3. See his protest against B. Weiss's discovery of a doctrine of election peculiar to James on the strength of James 2:5; *ibid.*, p. 78.

without a canon, there could be no normative biblical theology. It is obvious how influential this view expressed by Wrede was to become in the present century. (The essay of Stendahl, for example, makes a similar claim for the independence of historical study at the close of several decades of attempted theological re-construction.[4]) His abandonment of canon in the interests of historical research was resisted, however, by Adolf Schlatter, who believed that his challenge to New Testament Theology as a normative discipline needed to be met face to face. Schlatter accepted fully the scholarly obligation to historical work. He challenged Wrede's analysis in two important ways, however. First, he recognized that historical inquiry is not objective. Secondly, and consequently, the church's dogmatic task belongs inextricably together with its historical one. The picture of a church waiting patiently for the historians to complete their task before it knows what it can believe is false. Rather, the subject is as involved in the research as the object, and in the case of the believing historian he stands within a community which already relates to the historical material in a certain way. This is not just awkward inevitability, but belongs to the nature of the church, which must have 'dogma' because it must articulate 'what ideas have the right and the power to unite us'.[5] At this point the canon enters the argument again, for Schlatter sees it as expressing the fact that 'the New Testament history and the word which witnesses to it is the ground of Christianity's existence'.[6]

So the battle lines are drawn. Is history to have an autonomous right? Or is it to be governed by the teaching of the church? There are dangers in both sides. A history that presents itself too much on its objectivity will easily slip from under the authority of the Word: a scholarship that is strait-jacketed by a magisterium can learn, or at least say, nothing new. Schlatter saw that the way he advocated led across a tightrope, and that everything depended on balance. The

4. K. Stendahl, 'Biblical Theology, Contemporary', in *Interpreter's Dictionary of the Bible* 1, pp. 418–432, especially 425 ff.
5. A. Schlatter, 'The Theology of the New Testament and Dogmatics', in Morgan, *op. cit.*, p. 120.
6. *Ibid.*

problem still confronts the evangelical historian. How can one be 'open' yet also 'believing'? Schlatter's appeal for an honesty that is worthy of the name of 'scientific because it is self-aware is still pertinent.

Schlatter's legacy is hard to quantify. It is worth observing that he did not tie his argument about canon to a doctrine of inspiration.It is not impossible, furthermore, to read in him some degree of equivocation about the limits of the historian's independence.[7] It may be no surprise, therefore, that though he was himself conservative in his reading of the New Testament,[8] his appeal was not only to those of conservative inclination. Indeed, he was taken up with some enthusiasm by Bultmann (who was otherwise in the debt of Wrede), because of his stress on the contribution of the researcher's own world to the act of interpretation. Nevertheless, his perception that historical criticism should be pursued with all the rigour that was possible in the context of the believing community was salutary and, as I think we shall see, prophetic.

Theological Re-construction

In the decades following the First World War there were new attempts to come to terms with the problem of making theology out of the set of historical documents which form the Bible. These moved along different though related lines in Europe and America. The so-called Biblical Theology movement, as described by B.S. Childs,[9] was largely American, though it drew upon British and European scholars such as Eichrodt, Dodd and Rowley. Among the characteristics which forged it into something approximating to a 'movement' were its beliefs in revelation through history and the unity of the Bible. It is easy to see, therefore, why Eichrodt's two-volume *Theology of the Old Testament* should have been congenial to the Biblical Theology movement. His work stands at the beginning of the renaissance in European O.T. Theology, and bears marks of the influence of neo-orthodoxy. His aim was to avoid the opposite dangers of

7. *Ibid.*,p. 157.
8. *Cf.* Morgan's assessment, *ibid.*, p. 29.
9. B. S. Childs, *Biblical Theology in Crisis*, Philadelphia, 1970, pp. 13-87.

historicism and dogmatism (the goal which Schlatter had held out to theology). In pursuit of this, he constructed a theology in which both the unity of the Bible and historical criticism had a role.

Eichrodt's understanding of the unity of the Bible is more or less a matter of credo. In his attack upon historicism in the study of the O.T, he says that it 'could yet offer no serious substitute for the concept of the essential coherence of the Old and New Testaments'.[10] Consequently, he wrote a theology in which a key idea, covenant, enabled him to treat the scriptures as a unity. He believed that this theological schema was super-imposed by the borrowing of traditional categories in the manner trenchantly exposed by Wrede. In this connection the relation between theology and historical criticism in Eichrodt comes to the fore. He sees 'the historical principle operating side by side with the systematic in a complementary role,'[11] and applies at every point in his theology what he considers the results of historical criticism. The most important conjunction of history and theology occurs in connexion with covenant itself, when he argues for its entry into Israel's life at an early stage in her history. It is, indeed, established through the work of Moses, and moreover, emphasises 'the factual nature of the divine revelation'.[12] It is not wholly true to say with Kaiser, therefore, that Eichrodt's step from history to theology is a Kierkegaardian leap.[13] In his view of the centrality and reality of the Sinai event he has offered a reason based on a historical understanding (which incidentally ran counter to that which had prevailed in respect of covenant since Wellhausen) for constructing his theology in the way he did. The close interdependence of theology and history in Eichrodt is illustrated by the fact that Mendenhall's discovery of formal parallels between Hittite treaties and biblical covenantal texts

---

10. W. Eichrodt, *Theology of the Old Testament* 1, London, 1961, p. 30.
11. *Ibid.*, p. 32.
12. *Ibid.*, p. 37.
13. W. C. Kaiser, *Toward an Old Testament Theology*, Grand Rapids, 1978, p. 6.

lent a new impetus to Eichrodt's understanding of the centrality of covenant in biblical theology.[14]

Eichrodt marks an important step in our story of the twentieth century Old Testament Theology because he effectively followed the trail indicated by Schlatter in his decision to work within the confines of the canonical literature. His attempt to find a unifying principle in it is perhaps an extension of that decision. In the end he cannot escape the criticism that at many parts of his Theology the link between his allegedly central idea and the discussion of the individual matters is tenuous. Theology and criticism have a somewhat strained relationship in Eichrodt, therefore. He leaves a legacy that is somewhat forked. On the one hand he based his central theological principle firmly in a historical postulate. On the other, that postulate was subject to modification at the hands of changing fashions in biblical criticism. The point is made not to criticise Eichrodt, but to try to illustrate the dilemma that seems to be built into the task, as outlined by Schlatter, of doing theology and history together.[15] (Twenty years after the apppearance of Eichrodt's first volume, E.Jacob would recognise the need to construct his theology *provisionally* on what he took to be the prevailing critical understanding of Israel's literature and history.[16])

It may be said to follow from the above that Eichrodt's undisputed reign over the realm of O.T. Theology would end in due course, and indeed it was abruptly terminated by the appearance twenty years or so later of Von Rad's Old Testament Theology. von Rad apparently regarded the problems of basing theology on history as insoluble, and responded by postulating two 'histories', the one as reconstructed by scientific scholarship, the other the 'salvation-history' as believed and confessed by Israel and the legitimate basis of the church's confession.[17] The result was a separation between event and faith which has rightly been thought, if consistently applied, to be fatal to the latter.

14. Childs, *op. cit.*, p. 67.
15. Morgan criticises Schlatter for the same reason; *op. cit.*, p.33.
16. E. Jacob, *Theology of the Old Testament*, London, 1955, p.27.
17. G. von Rad, *Old Testament Theology* 1, Edinburgh, 1961, p. 107.

The differences between the methodologies of Eichrodt and von Rad, therefore, can hardly be over-estimated. To the former it was important to establish a historical basis for the faith proclaimed by Israel, and by extension the church; to the latter it did not, and indeed it could not in principle be done. Von Rad thus marked a turning-point in twentieth century O.T. Theology. It may not have been co-incidental that at approximately the same time the Biblical Theology movement was nearing the end of its course under heavy fire. Its belief in revelation through history is perhaps best known in G.E.Wright's *The God who Acts: Biblical Theology as Recital*.[18] The title may call to mind certain emphases of von Rad, but the thought is different. Wright is influenced by the conservative appreciations of Israel's history of Albright and Bright. It is important to him to be able to affirm that the faith of Israel was based on real events.The vulnerable point in the God-who-acts armour, found by Langdon Gilkey, was the reluctance of its wearers, under the influence of their devotion to a historical critical method, to allow any element of the miraculous in those precise events which they argued showed the might of God.[19] In seeking God in history it found, because of its own premises, that it could not be historical at all.

Perhaps, therefore, von Rad was right, and the only hope for theology was to cut it loose from history (*Historie*) altogether. However, von Rad's enterprise was not without its snags either. Two points may be made in particular. First, von Rad did not achieve so neat a separation between his scientific history and salvation-history as he wants to advocate. His picture of the developments in Israel's confession depends heavily on that of her history as it was widely understood when von Rad wrote. (There is a cursory but unqualified acknowledgement, in a footnote, of Martin Noth's work on Israel's origins, which has imposed itself in a thoroughgoing way on von Rad's delineation of Israel's

---

18. G. E. Wright, *The God who acts: Biblical Theology as Recital*, London, 1952.
19. L. Gilkey, 'Cosmology, Ontology and the Travail of Biblical Language', *Journal of Religion*, XLI, 1961, 194ff., especially p. 199.

earliest forms of belief.[20]) This is a further (negative) confirmation that the tasks of history and theology (as Schlatter insisted) belong inextricably together.

Secondly, like Eichrodt, von Rad works in practice with the canon of Scripture. This may at first appear to fit well with his understanding of the biblical literature as the confession of Israel and the church. However, though the structure of his theology derives in fact from a historical understanding (*viz* Noth's), there is a real tension between that fragmenting history and the unifying theological tendency betrayed by his adoption of the canonical literature and his reading of it according to a promise-fulfilment scheme. Von Rad may protest against the possiblity of any integrating theological principle, but he has actually imported the very thing. The form of his complete *Theology*, therefore, sits ill with its premises.These postulated a diversity of 'theologies'. The unity he discovers in the Bible as a whole hardly follows from them, but has been brought in by the theologian's fiat. Von Rad's separation of history and faith leaves an unbearable tension.

If the Biblical Theology movement failed to establish through historical criticism a historical basis for faith in the religion of Israel, von Rad failed to establish such a basis cut loose from historical criticism. It is not difficult, therefore, to understand the attractions of a theology of experience since about 1960, nor why Childs could write of the 'crisis' in biblical theology. It is to Childs that we turn next in our search for an adequate understanding of the relationship between history and theology.

Canonical Criticism
Brevard Childs' approach to the problem of relating history and theology is no longer very new, and the criticisms of it, spearheaded by James Barr, are well-rehearsed. Nevertheless, the method to which he gave impetus has to be our next calling-point, partly because the ideology is powerful, and because the discussion is still current, having grown inexorably out of previous endeavours. Childs himself has added to his pioneering work of Old Testament introduction

20. Von Rad, *op. cit.*, p. 107, n. 2.

an Introduction to the New Testament, and, most recently, his *Old Testament Theology in a Canonical Context*. So far in our study we have seen the need for theology to work within a canonical context stated by Schlatter and implicitly recognised both in European O.T. Theology and the Biblical Theology movement. In his latest work, and with his eye on both of these, Childs' carefully distances himself from all attempts to find hermeneutical keys to unlock the biblical message. The meaning of the Bible is not found by organising its material according to concepts, or reducing it to central truths (which might amount to the same thing); rather, 'the canon provides the arena in which the struggle for understanding takes place'.[21] This struggle for understanding happens, for Childs, with the use of all the methods and tools of historical criticism. His is an undertaking, therefore, precisely to do history and theology together. And his means of securing the rights of the theology of the church is to give paramount place to canon. In doing so he puts himself firmly in line with Reformation theology. 'To suggest (as he is doing) that the task of theological reflection takes place from within a canonical context assumes not only a received tradition, but faithful a disposition by hearers who await the illumination of God's spirit. This latter point has been developed so fully by Calvin as to make further elaboration unnecessary (*Institutes* 1, ch. 7)'.[22] Childs has apparently not quite returned to a doctrine of inspiration here, but it is very interesting that on canon he echoes Schlatter in such a way as to make his words sound like a prophecy finding their fulfilment.

Our question to Childs is whether his adoption of the canonical principle can solve the problem of relating theology and history. One of Barr's criticisms is that he replaced earlier attempts to find *theological* unifying principles with a merely formal one.[23] These do not seem to me to be mutually exclusive. However, the point as applied to Childs does have some validity. Like many of his predecessors he is concerned

21. B. S. Childs, *Old Testament Theology in a Canonical Context*, London, 1985, p. 15.
22. *Ibid.*, p. 12.
23. J. Barr, *Holy Scripture: Canon, Authority, Criticism*, Philadelphia, 1983, pp. 135f.

to demonstrate his commitment to historical criticism. (His desire to do constructive theology should not be construed as a return to fundamentalism; rather he hopes his way will be a bridge crossing the disastrous divides of times past.) It is in his understanding of the relationship between criticism and canonicity that problems arise.

The central problem is that the idea of canonicity is used in two different ways. On the one hand, canonisation bears its usual sense, namely the act of defining the extent of the literature to be regarded as authoritative within the community of faith. On the other hand, it refers to the process by which individual books come to take the form which they now possess. That process is subject to examination by the normal literary critical methods. For Childs, books come into their final form at the hands of a 'canonical' editor. This editor does not appear, from the point of view of historical investigation, to be very different from the 'final redactor' in common or garden redaction criticism. Childs denies this strenuously, arguing that a book is brought into its final form in and for a community, which thereby accepts the book as authoritative. However, this community is somewhat elusive, a figment defined by the text, and indeed a particular reading of the text. In practice the final redactor hypothesised by redaction criticism has become a canoniser with plenipotentiary powers to arbitrate among a variety of meanings which previous forms of the text may have borne, or impose new one. In Childs' idea of a 'canonical intentionality' he has, in fact, confused historical process with the act of canonising. The tell-tale phrase 'canonisation proper'[24] (referring to the latter) betrays the confusion in his use of the concept.

Childs' method, therefore, appears to secure the theological principle by the act of declaring the Bible the arena within which theological reflection should be done, and beyond that to leave the field clear to an autonomous historical criticism; whatever comes out at the end of the historical/'canonical' process is definitive and authoritative. His return to the canon, therefore, may be judged not fully to have taken up the challenge issued by Schlatter. Schlatter's call to a historical

24. Childs, *OTTCC*, p. 6.

criticism in a canonical context has implications for the way in which historical criticism is done. It contained *in nuce* a critique of historical criticism because of his understanding of the power of the subject in doing history. Addressing his contemporary situation, he says that the historian erroneously believes he can set aside his interests and do history objectively. But in reality: 'Historical investigations serve as weapons for the defence and attack of religious positions'.[25] Childs is not in fact oblivious to the philosophical loading of certain approaches to the biblical literature. He prefaces his treatment of revelation in his O.T. Theology with responses to the criticisms of the concept which come from analytical philosophy and sociological analysis. He also opposes certain classical critical formulations in the course of his work, *e.g.*, the old tendency to postulate religious evolution from lower (cultic) to higher (ethical) forms of religion.[26] It would be unjust to say, therefore, that his actual procedures are not governed by theological considerations. Nevertheless there is often such a discrepancy between the putative origin of a text and the way in which it comes to function in context that his method poses sharply the question as to the manner and locus of revelation.[27] Like canonisation, it seems to be virtually identical with the historical process.

It follows that the safeguarding of a real revelation in and through the biblical events is not achieved by the canonical principle alone, but requires a critical evaluation of the methods of criticism which are available to the interpreter. Two things may be observed even from a cursory survey of the field. First, and obviously, there are certain approaches which are explicitly opposed to the idea of a historical revelation. Bultman made no bones about his 'closed

---

25. Schlatter, *op. cit.*, p. 124.
26. Childs, *OTTCC*: on philosphical loading, pp. 20-26; on cultic-ethical evolution, p. 90.
27. For example, Childs, *ibid.*, p. 62, on the canonical placing of the decalogue, accepts its secondary character in that context, but does not address the implications of this revelation.

universe'.[28] We have already noticed Childs' opposition to sociological reductionism as in the work of N. K. Gottwald.[29] P. D. Hanson openly acknowledges his debt to Troeltsch, Mannheim and Weber.[30] A Hegelian postulate of conflict resolving itself into synthesis informs much of the detailed analysis of biblical books, as exemplified by the tensions found between the principles of law and grace in Deuteronomy in most modern commentaries.

The second characteristic of the field of biblical criticism is the power of consensus. This operates on several different levels. Most simply it relates to particular critical issues (such as the date of the arrival of the idea of covenant in Israel). It operates within critical 'schools' (Albright, Alt, Bultmann, Cullmann). And it is subject to broad changes of general approach. (The 'story' phenomenon enjoys some prominence at the time of writing.) Considerable pressure, therefore, is exerted upon the interpreter by his enviroment, both in the broad sense in terms of underlying assumptions about the scientific nature of the discipline and in the narrower sense in terms of perticular trends and influences. This factor is sometimes recognised by critical scholars as being inimical to the discovery of anything new.[31]

It follows from the recognition of the importance of consensus that many critical positions and procedures which seem impregnably strong are in reality fragile. They are open to challenge and correction and the proposal of new and different criteria. Just two particular points may be made in this connexion. First, the construction by critical scholarship of grand frameworks has led to an impression that much more

28. R. Bultmann, 'Is Exegesis without Presuppositions Possible', in S. Ogden, ed., *Existence and Faith*, New York, 1960, pp. 289—96 (especially p. 291).

29. N. K. Gottwald, *The Tribes of Yahweh*, London 1979.

30. P. D. Hanson, *The Dawn of Apocalyptic*, Philadelphia, 1970 (revised), pp. 211-220.

31. R. Rendtorff, in *Das Uberlieferungsgeschichtliche Problem des Pentateuch*, Berlin, de Gruyter, 1976, exposes the tenacious power of inherited ideas. In particular he laments the survival of the documentary hypothesis long after the advent of ideas in Old Testament studies which were fundamentally in tension with it; pp. 12-19.

is known about the flow of Israel's history and the development of her religion than is, on any sober estimate, the case. The existence of the framework allows individual pieces of the evidence to find convenient places within it. The exilic period, about which relatively little can be known with much confidence, has long been fruitful ground for theories about the burgeoning of Israelite religion.

An Evangelical Historical Criticism
Our sketch hitherto suggests that the course of biblical theology in this century has not run smooth. How may evangelical theologians respond to the real problems which we seen have rehearsed? First, it bears repeating that an openness is essential in any form of real historical enquiry. Having made the point it is necessary immediately to qualify it. Openness does not *only* mean being open to conclusions which do not suit the enquirer's viewpoint; it also means being open to the possibility of the unique event. For the historian, Old Testament theophanies and miracles are in principle analogous to the Resurrection for the New Testament scholar. By definition un-natural and extraordinary, it must elude confirmation by the normal means of historical investigation, and so must they. The evangelical theologian, however, though he cannot 'prove' the historicity of the Resurrection, will continue to affirm its historical character, since it is of the substance of the faith, and because historical investigation cannot show that it did *not* happen, except by ruling it out *a priori*. The analogy with the Resurrection has important consequences for the way in which the Old Testament theologian does his history. If the Resurrection is regarded as a non-negotiable historical basis for the faith, it may follow that the same will hold for certain Old Testament events (such as the Sinai theophany), perhaps with lesser degrees of necessity.

If this is so it will affect the evangelical interpreter's approach at almost every point. The point may be illustrated by reference to a widely used heuristic tool in Old Testament study, namely literary and theological similarity. It is almost axiomatic in biblical scholarship that similarity betrays dependence. This is often natural and uncontroversial, as when Jeremiah is said to have known the teaching of Hosea, or Ezekiel that of Jeremiah. In those cases one has independent historical data to apply. In other cases similarity is used to solve a problem. One such is that which exists between parts of the book of Jeremiah and the so-called deuteronomic literature, proving the late date of parts of Deuteronomy, and also the secondary character of large segments of Jeremiah by the postulate of a school marked out by characteristic style. This is a heavily literary procedure, of a kind which was actually criticised by Wrede for its failure to understand what is in any writer which produces a particular kind of expression. We can agree at least in a formal sense with Wrede here. The discovery in similarities of expression and ideas, answers to historical problems seems to presuppose a view of religion according to which it is created, as it were, from below. If, on the other hand, religious ideas are born in a word from God, then they might come, it seems to me, at different times, or apparently ahead of their time. The relationship between the origin of the idea and its expression in different kinds of literature will be a complex one. If this is so, literary and theological similarities cannot be used as a heuristic tool without some circumspection, and a large number of particular critical theories may have to be regarded with suspicion as a result.

It follows from the above that it is problematical simply to accept the (or a) prevailing critical consensus as the basis of an attempt to do Old Testament Theology. We saw earlier the general problem with doing so (the mobility of critical opinion), but have now added a problem of principle for the evangelical interpreter in particular. Any attempt to do biblical theology which wishes to remain broadly theologically orthodox but which tries to do justice to historical questions by locating itself on principle within the critical mainstream lays itself open to the suspicion of dualism.[32]

---

32. John Goldingay's recent perceptive book, *Theological Diversity and the Authority of The Old Testament*, Grand Rapids, 1987, would have contributed more to the discussion about history and criticism if it had recognised that many evangelical scholars and students have found it difficult to accept some of the central postulates of conventional Old Testament criticism.

It may need stressing again that I am not advocating abandonment of the historical task. That too is the way of dualism. I am asking for the recognition of certain limitations on the historian. In practice these involve a realism about the possibilities of historical research as applied to the Old Testament. Critical study has in general been too optimistic about its capacities to re-construct the history of Israel's religion. In fact, modesty, even a kind of agnosticism, are more appropriate. I cannot demonstrate that Moses declaimed Deuteronomy on the plains of Moab, but I might be willing to try to show the difficulties of supposing that the book only saw the light of day centuries later. On the other hand, there must be real cash-value to the commitment to openness. It is better to come honestly to unsought conclusions than to hide neurotically behind the cry, 'You can't prove it.'

I have been suggesting that a canonical principle alone is not sufficient to secure the interests of theology in the attempt to do the historical and theological tasks together. I believe it is necessary, and that Childs has rightly insisted that the crisis in biblical theology proved its necessity. Even after Childs, however, biblical theology seems to stand before a dilemma. Yet I think we have seen the ingredients of a more satisfactory way of approaching the question of theology and history.[33] It involves a commitment to work within the bounds of the canon. But it involves in addition a readiness to construct a critical methodology which does not compromise from the outset the revealed-ness of biblical religion. How is such a method to be constructed in a way that responds to Schlatter's call for honesty in the historical endeavour?

An important lead is given by W. C. Kaiser in his *Toward an Old Testament Theology*. Kaiser articulated principles which up to a point are similar to Childs', in that he defines the arena of biblical theology as the canon. However, he is

33. I have not attempted to draw Pannenberg into the discussion, as that would have taken us down a completely new avenue. However, I think that some of the observations just made about Eichrodt may apply also to Pannenberg, and that they certainly do to Rendtorff's contribution to *Revelation as History*, which rests on a highly tenuous interpretation of certain biblical passages; W. Pannenberg, ed., *Revelation as History*, New York and London, 1968; Rentorff's article, pp. 25–53.

different from Childs in two important respects. First, being in a theologically conservative tradition, he is openly critical of many of the methods used in mainstream historical criticism. Secondly, he has a broader understanding of the role of the canon in interpretation. As with Childs, the canon is not just a definition of limits, but has a kind of intentionality in its inner structure. Kaiser can speak of the 'canon's own view of things'.[34] His understanding of canonical intentionality, however, extends to the shape not just of individual books, but of the whole body of literature. Interestingly, Childs seems to be working towards something not very distant from this in his *OTTCC*, when he speaks of the 'intertextuality of the canon' to express the way in which its various parts relate together in mutual illumination.[35] In Childs' work we see increasingly, I think, that the canon has within itself the capacity to suggest the lines of its own interpretation.

Kaiser accepts this perspective at the outset. He speaks of an inductive approach to the identification of a key to the reading of Scripture. For him, if the shape of the canon means anything it means beginning at Genesis, and he proceeds via a discussion of Genesis 12:3, which he defends against allegations of lateness, and some broadly based lexicographical considerations, to his belief that promise is the category which can illuminate the purposes of God and unite all of Scripture.[36]

Kaiser's premises can be developed in a way which he, no doubt for practical reasons, has not taken. His *Theology* allows very little place for addressing critical questions. Indeed one important footnote, which challenges prevalent critical procedures in general terms, consigns that whole dimension of biblical study to the studies of Introduction and History of Religion rather than Theology.[37] No doubt these disciplines will remain separate because of the enormity of the task of combining them in any comprehensive way. Nevertheless, there is a special strength in studies of the sort

34. Kaiser, *op. cit.*, p. 35
35. Childs, *OTTCC*, p. 64
36. Kaiser, *op. cit.*, pp. 20–40.
37. *Ibid.*, p. 55.

which address critical questions at the same time as they aim to do constructive theology which does not limit itself to individual books of the Bible, but rather tries to bring out some of the interconnections between diverse parts of the canon. One book which illustrates the potential of such an endeavour is W.J. Dumbrell's *Covenant and Creation*,[38] in which the author takes on with exegetical precision the question of the composition of Genesis, even as he interprets the meaning of covenant in those early chapters. He goes on to develop the themes of covenant and creation across a wide range of biblical books, including the NT. There is considerable opportunity to build on this foundation. There has never been greater interest in the inter-relationship of parts of the Bible. The influence in recent times of the tendency to postulate basic conceptual unity in large tracts of the OT has been very great [39] The so-called 'story movement' also continues to be strong. These kinds of study are not always, indeed they are rarely, motivated by any explicit canonical concern.[40] Yet the are studies which the canonical material seems to have invited. current literature spawned by the 'story' movement in particular leaves perplexing questions unanswered. The emphasis falls so heavily on interconnections on the surface of the text, that historical questions are often not even addressed. Indeed the connections within and between biblical books can seem so sophisticated that the reader can be prompted to ask whether such artistry in conception is even compatible with historicity as it has usually ben understood by conservative theologians. In this new adventure in Old Testament studies there is both an invitation and a challenge to evangelical interpreters to think through how new discoveries about the text relate to the Old Testament's historicity claims.

38. W. J. Dumbrell, *Covenant and Creation*, Exeter, 1984.
39. *E.g.*, M. Noth, *The Deuteronomistic History*, Sheffield, 1981 (German, 1957).
40. An example is P. D. Miscall's *The Workings of Old Testament Narrative*, Philadelphia, 1983.

Conclusions

It is time to try to draw together some of the implications of our observations to this point

1. We began by arguing that a commitment to doing theology concertedly with history expressed itself naturally in a decision to do theology on the basis of the canonical literature, no more and no less. This commitment has been a feature whether implicitly or, as more recently, explicitly, of attempts to do biblical theology which have resisted the historicist programme of Wrede and others.

2. However, settling upon the canon as the proper arena of theological study is not in itself sufficient. Canonical Criticism indeed contains within itself deep ambivalences, and needs to be augmented by an evaluative approach to critical methods. This approach affirms the need for the historical task to be done in tandem with the theological, in mutual regulation It recognises the importance of the role of the subject in doing history. Justice is not done to the full extent of that role by an appeal to 'hermeneutics' as a mediating process, as that can leave the autonomy of historical criticism intact.

3. The shape and inner structuring of the canonical literature itself can give pointers towards the building of a biblical theology. The emergent theological concerns of the literature will contribute to decision-making about matters which might be regarded as properly the province of historical criticism (such as the historicity of the patriarchal narratives or of Jonah).

4. The theology in question will have respect to the inter-relationships of the various parts. In this respect Kaiser's 'Analogy of Antecedent Scripture' places an unwarranted constraint on the ways in which the parts of canonical literature may inter-relate. Childs' 'intertextuality' is more promising, if elusive. In reality our canonical theology is driving us back, willy-nilly, to something akin to an *analogia fidei* informed by the insights of that contemporary criticism which has demonstrated the complexity of the inter-relationships between books and parts of books.

5. Finally, the foregoing welcomes a particular approach to the doing of biblical theology. Short of the *magnum opus* which will successfully perform all the historical work required to support a biblical theology based on the premises

outlined, there are avenues open for thematic studies which break the moulds both of the commentary format and of the 'digest' theology. These would do their historical criticism, be aware of the inter-relationships between books, and perhaps be the fruit of dialogue between biblical and dogmatic scholarship.

CHRIST AND HISTORY: AN EARLY VERSION

Roy Kearsley

Many current disagreements in theology stem from a prior view of the status of history, and particularly fundamental to a Christian understanding are questions concerning whether history is the field of divine providence, is a mode of revelation, is even a rational continuum with direction and goal. These questions arise, it seems, before bolder ones about the status of the biblical salvation-events themselves both as significant rational historical occurrences and as determinants of subsequent history. Even the vexed question of the 'Christ of faith' and 'Jesus of history' looks to such prior considerations.

There is still some merit in examining early Christian tradition to see how much it anticipated this debate, despite the common assumption that such a cultural and conceptual gulf separates modern theological thought from early "Christian writers that second-century views will yield nothing relevant for today. For an age that could produce a Celsus is not so very far from our own[1] and whilst we yet await concensus on whether ancient Platonised schemes promoted *cyclic* views of history and cosmology[2], we can say that most of them operated with an assumed *self-contained* universe. This is surely a remarkably modern idea relevant to the status of

1. See C. Brown, *Miracles and the Critical Mind*, London, 1984, pp. 5, 6; C. Gunton, *Yesterday and Today*, London, 1983, pp. 110, 118; R. P. C. Hanson, *Studies in Christian Antiquity*, Edinburgh, 1985, pp. 3-20.
2. Those who think they did include E. Bevan, *Hellenism and Christianity*, London, 1921, p. 123; C. N. Cochrane, *Christianity and Classical Culture*, NY/Oxford, 1957, pp. 483-484; J. Daniélou, *The Lord of History, Reflections on the Inner Meaning of History*, London, 1958, p. 1; C. Dawson, 'The Christian View of History', in C. T. McIntyre (Ed.), *God, History and Historians: An Anthology of Modern Christian Views of History*, NY/Oxford, 1977, pp. 29-45. A contrary view is held by G. L. Patterson, *God and History in Early Christian Thought, A Study of Themes from Justin Martyr to Gregory the Great*, London, 1967, pp. 156-157.

history and one that, in various guises, persists in modern Christian thought.

Amongst second-century writers, Justin and Irenaeus stand out from the pack as representatives of early thinking. Did these two seminal thinkers treat history as a continuum of events which are rationally significant, both in themselves and as part of a larger process and did they place salvation-history astride human history in general? The latter question is especially important since modern debate sometimes asks whether these two 'histories' form independent spheres which may only sometimes interact, as argued by Daniélou and the historian Butterworth, or whether Christian history or 'salvation-history' in some measure directs subsequent history in general. As chief apologists for Christianity in the second century, Justin and Irenaeus should reflect the more thoughtful and moderate versions of a Christian dogma of history.

JUSTIN MARTYR

The matter of greatest importance for Justin is salvation through the discovery of truth which, for him, cannot be an end in itself but issues in the remission of sins. Too much can be read into the opening narrative of the *Dialogue* where Justin relates his pilgrimage through various philosophical schools before finally finding the truth in Christianity. This is a natural opening gambit, given the apologetic nature of the writing but it must not be taken to characterise his Christian faith as merely, or even primarily, a superior philosophy. The real thrust of his appeal is soteriological and issues from a concrete history:

> It becomes you to move quickly to know in what way forgiveness of sins and a hope of inheriting the promised good thins, shall be yours. But there is no other way than this: to become acquainted with this Christ, to be washed in the fountain spoken of Isaiah for the remission of sins. (*Dial. 44*)

The stress falls not upon some rational scheme of truth but upon attention to an event historically verifiable to Christians and non-Christians alike, namely the crucifixion. It is the first theme by which we shall focus up Justin's handling of history and is the most striking. In some measure, of course, its persistence emanates from the defence against Jewish probes. Trypho the Jew finds a crucified messiah one of the indigestible pieces of Christian teaching *(Dial. 89)* and it is significant that discussion of the cross is fuller in the *Dialogue* than in the *Apologies.* Yet the occurrences in the *Apologies* are significant. Amongst the OT predictions which vindicate the Christian faith those relating to the cross have decisive significance. They depict Christ as cosmic lord, reigning from the tree *(I Apol. 1.41).* In his final summing-up of the case from prophecy the cross emerges as more than the cosmic cipher or symbol elaborated in *I Apol. 55* and *Dialogue 89, 90.* Rather it is an *historical* datum, held to tenaciously whatever the problems it raises:

> For with what reason should we believe of a crucified man that he is the first-born of the unbegotten God . . . unless we had found testimonies concerning him published before he came . . . and unless we saw that things had happened accordingly. *(I Apol. 1.53)*

In *I Apol. 1.51* the cross fixes the significance even of the incarnation. An accompanying reference to Pontius Pilate underlines its historical value. In the *Dialogue* it assumes the heady status of a dispensation or arrangement in the order of the divine plan, a *special* kind of historical event *(Dial. 30, 45, 103).* On occasion, Justin is prepared to identify the cross alone as *the* redeeming event *(Dial. 86).*

Justin accented the cross precisely as event awarding it cosmic significance as an objective occurrence which settles the course of wider history. The idea of the cosmic cross, according to J. Daniélou, is that:

> its shape suggests a cosmic symbolism, expressing the universality of the redemptive act by unifying all things, giving solidity to the new creation.[3]

3. J. Daniélou, *Theologie du Judeo-Christianisme,* Paris, 1958, p. 289, quoted in E. F. Osborn, *Justin Martyr (Beitrage Zur Historischen Theologie)* (Ed. G. Ebeling), Tubingen, 1973, p. 52.

Further, Justin underpinned the objectivity by an occasional vicarious interpretation of Christ's work on the cross which invested the event with a yet greater decisiveness. He even built on the notion of curse-bearing. The curse pronounced upon Israel for failure to keep the law should, he alleged, fall even more certainly upon the Gentile nations. But,

> the Father of all wished his Christ for the whole human family to take upon him the curses of all . . . caused him to suffer these things in behalf of the human family . . . that by his stripes the human race might be healed . . . the statement in the law: "Cursed is every one that hangs on a tree" confirms our hope which depends upon the crucified Christ. *(Dial. 95, 96).*

Admittedly, we do not have here a common theme in Justin but it is a determinative one, placed moreover in interdependent relation with other important notions, giving it an integrated status. For instance, the celebrated combative tone of early soteriology, the so-called 'dramatic idea of victory over the devil, is precisely Justin's concern here. God has diverted his curse from people and,

> declared that he would break the power of the serpent and would bring to those who believe in him who was to be crucified, salvation from the fangs of the serpent, which are wicked deeds, idolatries, and other unrighteous acts. *(Dial. 91)*

So the taking of the curse by Christ in his crucifixion formed the *mechanism* for defeating evil. In this way the event of the cross took hold of human history. It removed the burden of curse from the whole human family and assumed pivotal significance. It was a watershed in all human history, precisely because it combatted a universal curse and thereby a universal enemy. For Justin Christian exorcism bore out this conclusion. By it, 'demons are subdued to his name and to the dispensation of his suffering' *(Dial. 30).* In the same way',

The concealed power of God was in Christ the crucified, before whom demons, and all the principalities and powers of the earth tremble. *(Dial. 49)*

We may have here the key to the striking depiction of Christ 'reigning from the tree'. A special kind of event has surged into history tipping the scales of conflict and decisively breaking the power of evil.

Behind Justin's treatment of history in relation to salvation lies the centrality of the incarnation. The apologist repeatedly emphasises the unique manner of Christ's generation. Jesus had an 'ineffable origin' *(I Apol. 51)* but, startlingly, is one 'not having descent from men. . . .' *(Dial 63)* and whose 'blood did not spring from the seed of man. . . .' Even, it is said, '. . . he appeared and was man but not of human seed', *(Dial. 76)* and denied that he is 'man of men' *(Dial. 48)*. It will transpire that Justin believes fully in the humanity of Jesus and so here is only fending off the Ebionite denial of the virgin birth. The effect, however, is to heighten the sense of divine incursion into human affairs, into the human story.

But another history-shaping component surfaces in Justin's thought. Plainly, to him the *incarnation,* like the cross, forms a critical, unique and decisive event. He adopts two methods of installing the incarnation in the cockpit of history. The first is by insisting that everything, but especially the axis events of virgin birth and crucifixion were predicted by the prophets *(I Apol. 31-36, 53, Dial. 7 et passim)*. The coming of the Word into human history marks the climax, the peaking of a well-established flow of revelation. It is not dislocated from God's saving moment in Jewish history but rather sums it up and crowns it.[4]

The cross to which the incarnation carried Christ was indeed a special *oikonomia* dispensation or phase, having its own discrete significance. But probably quite another, though connected, sense of the *oikonomia* appears in *Dialogue 67,* where the suffering of Christ 'completes the dispensation'. Christ rounds off and completes the era of the law, though completely continuous with it.

4. *Cf.* E. F. Osborn, op. cit. p. 156.

Justin argues for the continuity and cohesion of the work of God. On the other hand he is sure that Christ does not merely continue but consummates the dispensation. He rounds off . . . completes the work begun at the creation.[5]

This duality of use of the *oikonomia* (that is, for both individual event and for era) is important for it illustrates both Justin's belief in the decisive significance of individual saving events and also their full significance only within the flow of saving history. These events are organically connected and therefore fully coherent only within the series. The virgin birth is here a vital element for maintaining a *physical* unity within the history of salvation and therefore crops up particularly in predictive prophecy.

The second way that Justin locates the incarnation within the flow of history is by reference to the *Logos Spermatikos*. The definitive article by Holte[6] on this is widely cited and I need not attempt to catalogue his points. Briefly summarised, he finds that Justin's treatment of this Stoic theme in the key passages conceives of the *Logos Spermatikos* not primarily as a material and pantheistic portion of the Logos belonging to all human beings but a universal faculty by means of which the Logos radiates the knowledge of himself in a somewhat fragmentary way upon all wise and perceptive philosophers. This knowledge, however, is complete only through the revelation of the incarnate Logos who carries a *dunamis* for awakening every kind of human being – not just those, like Socrates, with a special capacity to receive it. Here again Justin has succeeded in blending the unique significance of the incarnation, its special potency within the flow of the human story, with its continuity in the greater activity of the God in human affairs. In this brilliant presentation, the apologist turns a concept of constancy into a term also of unique departure. His treatment of the OT as a salvation-history culminating in Christ as both climax and new beginning through a second

5. *Ibid.,* p.40.
6. Ragnar Holte, 'Logos Spermatikos: Christianity and Ancient Philosophy according to St Justin's Apologies'.,in *Studia Theologia XII,* 1958, 109-168.

Eve *(Dial. 100)*[7] is now transplanted into the Gentile world of thought. But even there it retains the same sense of decisiveness, of no turning back or choosing the past again.

Finally, just as Justin drew out a history leading up to the incarnation and the cross he also envisaged one leading away from it, ingeniously harnessing the illumination motif as a soteriological theme. It is sometimes overlooked that the illumination or enlightenment brought by the Word extended, for Justin, to his own time and beyond, to the contemporary phase of the saving programme. It occurred in the ongoing flow of the history of salvation through Christian conversion. We are dealing, in other words, with the subjective aspect of atonement which is not restricted to some decisive event of history but moves in the flow of history, that is, the events of conversion *(Dial. 7, 8 cf. I Apol. 23)* and baptism *(I Apol. 61)*. This is the main point, I suggest, behind Justin's remark that 'we actually see things that have happened and are happening as predicted. . . .' *(I Apol. 30)* It is in this sense that Christians are still witnesses to the redemptive events which mark the fulfilment of OT promise. Christ summons people to a new blessing in a new Canaan promising a new friendship with God. It is universal, extensive, everlasting and incorruptible and finally can only shatter the limits of the present historical order *(Dial. 139 cf. 113)*.

In summary we can say that Justin believed in the rational significance, the *oikonomia*-quality both of saving history as a whole and of special events in particular, especially the virgin birth and the cross. He saw these axis events as determinants of ensuing human history and as indicating continuity, departure, completion and a new contemporaniety for all ages with the salvation era.

IRENAEUS

In Irenaeus we find a much more developed soteriology than that in Justin, due in great measure to the challenge offered by the Gnostic way of salvation. Irenaeus is obliged to show what is the *true* origin, destiny and quest of the human race amidst its history. The question of destiny, as is well known, he handles with a markedly mystical approach in

---

7.   See also Osborn, *op. cit.* 156.

which humanity rises by degrees to partake of divine immortality, the vision of God, and likeness to God (especially *Adv. Haer. 3.11.5; 3.18.7; 4.14.1; 4.20.5; 4.38.3; Dem. 31, 40).*

Simon Tugwell believes that the goal in mind is, for Irenaeus, the direct opposite of the Gnostic vision, not the realisation of the immaterial soul but the elevation of the body so that it might enjoy union with God. Couching the matter in what Tugwell calls the 'myth' of man growing as a child to adulthood emphasises that such a union will *take time to achieve* and is the climax of the divine creative activity. Creation occupies, therefore, according to Tugwell, 'the whole of time from the beginning of the world to the end'.[8] The Irenaean scheme, then, is not merely *amenable* to the notion of a progressive human history directed towards the divinely conceived goal. It *requires* a history, and a long one at that.

The role of the Son of God in this divinisation, highlighted by illumination and nourishment imagery, underpins that idea of process and of time's passage. The Son of God remains in human history drawing afresh the story of the human quest, and the vision that ultimately brings incorruptibility has a power which precedes the eschaton. For Irenaeus it is a present, sustained pursuit. The gifts and revelations of God, according to *Adv. Haer. 4.20, 7* are directed by the Son from the beginning, in an orderly and systematic fashion at appropriate times, for only with proper attention to time can the revelation be fruitful.

This same activity is anticipated in the work of the prophets,

> that man might be formed beforehand and exercised in appropriating to himself that glory which shall be afterwards revealed to them that love God. (*Adv. Haer. 4.20,7*)

Preparation for the saving sight of God, an activity of the Son of God under the old covenant, therefore invades the

---

8. S. Tugwell 'Irenaeus and the Gnostic Challenge', *The Clergy Review,* 66, 1981, (pp. 127-130, 135-137), pp. 135-6.

present as he becomes known in this era. It belongs to continuous pre-eschaton history. This thought emerges in various ways through several of Irenaeus' salvation themes. In the well-known recapitulation approach *(Adv. Haer. 1.10.1; 2.12.4; 3.16.6; 3.18.1; 3.18.7; 3.19.1; 4.14.1)* the human race needs prolonged time and history to pass through the stages of progress to adulthood. It is a training which takes time. Humanity must grow, multiply, grow in strength, be glorified and having been glorified only then see God *(Adv. Haer. 4.38.3)*. It is only after much progress that mankind will become incorruptible.[9] No such process could now take place, however, without a new phase of history, the winning of a decisive reversal in human affairs. Iranaeus says that in fact such has occurred in the generation not only of a new Adam but also of a new Eve. It is in the fullness of time that God sends his second Adam born of a woman, marking his gathering-up of all things by entry through a woman *(Adv. Haer. 5.21.1 cf. 5.19.11)*. There arises, therefore, a new phase in history, a new start and a new generation, but a fully human one. It is both irreversible and invincible and after this second Adam nothing can be the same again. This crucial notion secures an influence for salvation-history over all subsequent history in general.

At this point another feature of Irenaeus' thought becomes relevant. The well-known victory motif, having its own bearing on the question of history, surfaces out of the recapitulation theory. The successful obedience of Jesus resonates as a great triumph by the Word on behalf of the human race as in, for example, *Adv. Haer. 3.18.6*, where Christ wrestles and overcomes as a man contending for his fathers paying the debt of disobedience by his obedience and so binding the strong man *(Adv. Haer. 3.18.7)*. However, that is not all, since the decisive victory of the 'Champion' does not eliminate the need for a perpetuated achievement in time and history. The prize of incorruption will be won by struggle in the individual *(Adv. Haer. 4.37.7)* but, more significantly, in the church for,

9. F. Altermath, 'The Purpose of the Incarnation according to Irenaeus', in E. A. Livingstone (Ed.), *Studia Patristica XIII, Part II*, Berlin, 1975 (pp. 63-68), p. 65, citing *Adv. Haer. 5.9.2.*

God for his part displaying long-suffering ... that ... the church (may) be shaped after the manner of his Son's image and *so at last* man may attain his full growth, ripening ... for the sight and comprehension of God.

Adulthood, adoption and immortality in communion with God still need time to mature. Once again the scheme of salvation requires the flow of history, and a lengthy history at that, to work itself out. However, the *decisiveness* and *finality* of Christ's victorious obedience lies, for Irenaeus, ultimately in the climax of the cross. It is not strictly true to say that for Irenaeus the cross was only <u>an</u> event in the life of Christ not *the* event.[10] He frequently isolates the cross (or the 'passion') as *the* redeeming event *(Adv. Haer. 2.20.2; 3.5.3; 3.16.9; 4.2.7; 5.2.1,2; 5.14.3,4; 5.16.3; 5.17.1; 5.23.2)*. It is surely not enough to explain this tendency by simply saying that Irenaeus saw the cross as the crowning act of obedience, though this is certainly true *(Dem. 34)*. For one thing, the connection of ransom and blood in some of these passages certainly makes the notion of a ransom price unavoidable. Equally, the one passage which speaks of propitiation *(Adv. Haer. 5.17.1)* is not easily evaded. At the very least, it fixes the cross at the turning point of the human story:

And therefore in the last times the Lord has restored us into friendship through his incarnation, having become 'the Mediator between God and men', propitiating indeed for us the Father against whom we had sinned and cancelling our disobedience by his own obedience.

Moreover, in another passage *(Dem. 69)* Irenaeus speaks of Christ taking judgment upon himself and in the process removing it from others, though there is some doubt about the precise form of the text. At any rate, once again the cross is decisive in the salvation story. Like Justin, Irenaeus gives a universal significance to the cross *(Dem. 34)* and it becomes a sign of God's empire and continuing government *(Dem. 84)*.

10. J. Lawson, *The Biblical Theology of St Irenaeus*, London, 1948, citing Beuzart, p. 187.

The impact of the cross in these terms is more than subjective and individualistic. It reaches into the cosmos and leaves an indelible mark there:

> And because he is himself the Word of God Almighty, who in his invisible form pervades us universally in the whole world, and encompasses both its length and breadth in height and depth – for by God's Word everything *is disposed and administered* – the Son of God was also crucified in these, imprinted in the form of a cross on the universe; for he had necessarily, in becoming visible, to bring to light the universality of his cross, in order to show openly through his visible form *that activity* of his. . . . *(Proof 34)*

This is a difficult passage to interpret and other translations have been offered of some of the more crucial parts.[11] Almost certainly, however, the influence of Justin's 'cosmic cross' is to be felt here, or at least some commonly held tradition. At any rate, the thrust seems not to be a kind of Platonic idealism, conceiving the cross as some supra-historical principle hidden in the eternal and transcendent Word. Rather, it has to do with the Word's *government* and direction of all things. The cross is a decisive and determinative element, it seems even *the* determinative element, in that government. The universality of the form of the cross bears silent witness to this but it is only with the incarnation and the actual event of the cross that the disposing power of the cross is perceived just as the first tree, the tree of the knowledge of good and evil produced a fateful and lasting result. The cross sets off a whole new direction in history, powerful enough, in Irenaeus' view, to direct human destiny to its goal. Of course, the resurrection carries Christ through the distress and places him at the helm of history as both king and judge, '. . . who *rises to rule over the nations* . . . to be acknowledged as Son of God and king' (Dem. 61). After the general resurrection Christ would rise to be judge of the whole world and the only worker of justice and redemption. This, along with the context of the millenium

---

11. See Smith, *op. cit.,* pp. 172-173.

theme, illustrates how directly Irenaeus moved from the cross and resurrection to Christ's domination of history. For him the events inaugurated a permanent durable renovation: 'He fulfilled all things by his advent and he is still fulfilling them in the church until the consummation. . . .' (*Adv. Haer.* 4.56.1)[12] He was bound in any case to arrive at this point by his discussion of the two trees, the two Adams, and the two Eves. These coupled subjects point to a double historical axis profoundly determinative for the human condition and human events. Into the picture now comes the incarnation itself and its significance for history in Irenaeus' thought.

At the outset we must recognise some ambiguity in Irenaeus. There is his feeling for a direction in human history, of human growth and God's activity in it to the extent of determining it merely by the entry of the Word as flesh and blood to realise the chosen goal (*Adv. Haer. 3.19.1*). Yet he also perceives a disruption in history so the entry of the Word does not simply impel along a consistent path but also restores what has been lost, renovates in the midst of a history which has lost its way (*Adv., Haer. 3.10.2; 3.18.1; 5.14.1-3*).

What must certainly be clear to students of Irenaeus is his conviction that the incarnation marks a decisive epoch in human history, the beginning of the 'last times' (*Adv. Haer. 3.5.3*). Christ is he who was became a man among men in the last times (*Adv. Haer. 4.20.5*). This period signals the 'end of times' (*Dem. 18 et passim*) and the fullness of time (*Adv. Haer. 3.17.4; 4.20.7*), and is all part of the divinely foreordained order of time and events (*Adv. Haer. 4.20.7*). The incarnation and life of the Word amongst mankind was itself the fulfilling of the *oikonomia* or administration of humanity (*Adv. Haer. 3.17.4*). So, for Irenaeus, 'The incarnation was . . . the great climax of the history of the human race'.[13] According to Irenaeus all who from the beginning of human history feared and loved God prefigured

---

12. Van den Brink comments, 'The renewal, is not . . . an event of one albeit decisive moment, now passed and consolidated in a doctrine. The renewal . . . is permanent and durable today. . .' in E. A. Livingstone (Ed.), 'Reconciliation in the Fathers', *Studia Patristica XIII, Part II,* Berlin 1975 (pp 90-106), p. 95

13. Lawson, *op. cit.* pp. 172-173.

the church and were one with it *(Adv. Haer. 4.17.2)*. But that is not all. Although it was a climax of history it was also the *beginning* of a history, the unfolding of what is contained in the OT about the end-time *(Adv. Haer. 1.10.3)*.

There is, then, continuity in history from the former to the last times. Echoes of Justin's *Logos Spermatikos* are to be heard in Irenaeus: 'His Word . . . who is ever present with mankind, united and blended with his own creative . . . and made flesh is Jesus Christ. . . .' *(Adv. Haer. 3.17.6)* The incarnation, however, is a decisive and definite event. It marks the beginning of the 'year of the Lord', the distinct period running from the incarnation to the consummation in which people are 'called and saved by the Lord', and which is the 'time of faith' *(Adv. Haer. 2.12.2)*. This period, however is not a mere eddy or creek, slipped off from the mainstream of human affairs. It is that which culminates in the day of recompense, the 'day' that follows upon the 'year of the Lord' *(Adv. Haer. 2.12.2)*. When the 'year' finishes, a new heaven and earth begins *(Adv. Haer. 36.1.3)*.

So the role of the Word in the historical process enjoys an all-inclusive character. He is the Word who governs the cosmos in its beginning, in the whole period leading up to the incarnation, in the era leading away from that event, and in its culmination:

Son of God . . . born before all the building of the world and appearing to the whole world in the end of this age as man, the Word of God *resuming anew in himself all things in heaven and earth. (Dem 30)*

The *recapitulatio* inaugurated by the incarnation reaches right out to a total and exhaustive climax of human history. The present age of the church, for Irenaeus, is the time of the human race's pilgrimage towards that consummation. There can be no question of the historical era of the church, or the 'year of the Lord', being a detached parallel history, or a history within a history, some kind of sideshow. For Irenaeus, according to J. Daniélou, '. . . the history of salvation embraces not only the history of mankind, but the whole of cosmic history'.[14] It should perhaps be noted that Daniélou does not himself believe that the church should view itself as the stimulus for social progress or political innovation. He holds the real purpose of history to be the production of human personalities and the sacred and secular history to be really independent of each other.[15] In contrast, C. Dawson comments that Gnostic ideas contained the notion of an eternally recurrent process of history in the cosmic cycle and that against this Irenaeus asserted the uniqueness of the Christian revelation and *the necessary relation between the divine unity and the unity of history,* of 'one human race in which themysteries of God are worked out'.[16] In conclusion, then, whatever problems we find with Irenaeus' view today, he certainly saw history as a continuum and he invested individual events with a rational significance. Moreover, for him the history of God's saving work was determinative of the direction of history as a whole. At that early and fragile stage of the church's existence he had even less encouragement in this conviction than some may think we have today, faced as we are with the ambiguity of history. This can only mean that the conviction arose from his reflection on the church's primary documents and doctrinal tradition, and belongs to the network of primal Christian ideas.

CONCLUSION

G. L. Patterson argued that one aspect of the achievement of early Christian writers was to elevate a particular course of events to a matter of *rational* concern, something which contemporary chroniclers of events failed to do.[17]

This review of two dominant figures of second-century Christian thought seems to confirm his judgment. For both of them, all of human history was the domain of the Word both up to and after the NT saving events. These events, significant in themselves, were embedded in the continuities of history but also marked a determinative departure which enfolded all

14. J. Daniélou, *The Lord of History,* op. cit, p. 28.
15. Ibid., pp. 101-104.
16. C. Dawson, 'The Christian View of History', in C. T. McIntyre, *op. cit.* (pp. 29-45), p. 32.
17. G. L. Patterson, *op. cit. ,* p. 29.

the subsequent human story within itself. With regard to the question which we raised in passing concerning the modern distinction between the Christ of faith and the Jesus of history this was plainly not an axiom natural to second-century thinking. Of course it would be hunting anachronisms to search for it there in such a form, and in any case the writers were only two or three generations on from the apostles, possessing a faith still fresh in its historical roots. This said, however, Justin and Irenaeus attached historically determinative significance to the career of Jesus, and armed with its detailed history persistently made demands upon their readers' faith. They did this to such a degree that it is difficult to know in what form their theology could have borne the weight of the modern idea.

BIBLICAL NARRATIVE AND HISTORICAL REFERENCE

Henri Blocher

After the eclipse, a more glorious blaze! Since Hans Frei, of Yale, published his book *The Eclipse of Biblical Narrative*,[1] attention has focused on this kind of discourse in the Bible, and the topic has come to outshine other stars of the academic firmament. A new brand of theology, with unusual attractive power, goes by the name of 'Narrative theology'.

The fatigue of the older historical-critical method called for it: dissatisfaction with the barrenness of endless source-analysis and dubious reconstructions. The new approach continues in the way of literary *genres* study, which Roman Catholic scholars, especially, such as André Robert, happily pursued in the decades after World War II, but it does so on a larger scale, with finer tools, and fervent passion. As a discipline which applies a specific methodology, it may be called 'rhetorical criticism'. Much of the impetus, of course, has come from the flourish of secular literary criticism. The 'big name' here is that of the most famous literary critic in the world, Northrop Frye of Toronto. Borrowing for its title a designation of the Scriptures which William Blake had coined, Frye crowned his career with the writing of an original survey, full of provocative ideas, in its own manner a monument of the narrative treatment: *The Great Code: The Bible and Literature*.[2] Side-effects of the vogue of structuralism also had a part: concentration on the text as it is, in its wholeness, and above all in its form, disinterest in authorial intent and reality beyond, are shared by both

1. Hans W. Frei, *The Eclipse of Biblical Narrative. A Study in Eighteenth and Nineteenth Century Hermeneutics*, Newhaven & London: Yale University Press, 1974, 355 pp.
2. Northrop Frye, *The Great Code. The Bible and Literature*, Harcourt, Brace, & Jovanovitch Publishers, 1982, translated into French by Catherine Malamoud, *Le Grand Code. La Bible et la littérature*, Paris: Seuil, 1984, 345 pp. Unfortunately, for want of a copy of the English original, we shall quote from the French edition, and, oddly, we shall have to retranslate Frye's words from the French.

currents.[3] The on-going debate on hermeneutics, which
Bultmann's *Entmythologisierung* spurred in the forties,
naturally flows into the newly opened spaces; narrative
theology offers avatars of much that was said about Biblical
myths (a term which N. Frye cherishes), and philosophical
hermeneutics of the post-Bultmannian era, majoring as they
do on language, have taken hold of the narrative theme. We
acknowledge here as the master of Masters Paul Ricoeur, with
the *magnum opus Temps et récit*[4] and the collection of essays
Du texte `a l'action.[5]

Regarding its relationship to tenets, or habits, of evangelical
theology, comments vary. As he champions viewing the Bible
as literature, James Barr avails himself of the opportunity to
deride once more the Fundamentalists' obsession with 'facts':
they continue fighting an obsolete battle, they miss the point,
they do not see that the proper category is story, not history.[6]
Others, on the contrary, try to woo evangelical readers and to
persuade them that narrative theology sufficiently meets the
demands of orthodoxy. With great conviction and high hopes,
Mark Ellingsen opened his arms and set forth a major plea to
this purpose, a few years ago.[7] Even the confession of
infallibility, he claims, can find its legitimate place within the
new frame: for the texts function infallibly within the
Christian language-game.[8] Donald Carson, however, warns
that the label 'literary tool' is potentially deceptive, and he
fears that indifference to the external referents in rhetorical
criticism do away with 'the scandal of particularity' inherent

---

3. Melvin Tinker, *The Bible as Literature. The Implications of
   Structuralism*, Leicester: Theological Students Fellowship, 1987,
   35, referring to John Barton, *Reading the Old Testament*, DLT,
   1984.
4. Paul Ricoeur, *Temps et récit*, Paris: Seuil, 1983-1985, 3 volumes.
5. Paul Ricoeur, *Du Texte `a l'action Essais d'herméneutique*, II, Paris:
   Seuil, 1986, 414 pp.
6. James Barr, *Fundamentalism*, London: SCM, 1977, 179; 'Story and
   History in Biblical Theology', *Journal of Religion* 56, 1976, 1-17
7. Mark Ellingsen, 'Should Philosophical Theories about History
   Divide Christ's Body? Narrative Hermeneutics as an Orthodox
   Alternative', *Evangelium-Gospel* 3, 1985, 82-99, notes 100–109.
8. *Ibid.*, 97.

in the revelation of the self-incarnating God'.[9] Part of a brilliant essay in the same symposium, by Kevin J. Vanhoozer scrutinizes this point, with help drawn from Austin's and Searle's speech-act theory;[10] a similar undergirding gives strength to *The Responsibility of Hermeneutics*, a most significant work by R. Lundin, A. C. Thiselton, and C. Walhout.[11] Without hiding behind their competence, we have an ambition to follow in their footsteps, narrative *theology* being more precisely on our mind, and to add a few remarks as can be made from the side of evangelical dogmatics.

We shall follow a three-part outline: the simpler, the better. We shall give, first, a sketchy account of the narrative approach; we shall, then, attempt to score the positive points; but we shall express reservations, thirdly, on the fate of historical reference at the narrativists' hands. *Grosso modo*, we welcome narrative theology in what it affirms, but we would resist it, resist it strenuously, in what it denies or disregards.

Scripture as story

Hans Frei's *Eclipse of Biblical Narrative*, to start again with it, is no treatise on method: it is a piece, a large piece, of historical research. The sub-title reads: 'A Study in Eighteenth and Nineteenth Century Hermeneutics'. What it revealed was the price paid for the rise and reign of historical-critical 'science'. What it gained, it gained at the expense of the appropriation of what the texts really say. The Reformers and the older Protestants were able to receive fully the language of the Bible, to let it shape their thought and life, without setting apart its historical reference; 'the Bible was a coherent world of discourse in its own right, whose depictions and teachings

9. D. A. Carson, 'Recent Developments in the Doctrine of Scripture', in the symposium jointly edited with John D. Woodbridge, *Hermeneutics, Authority and Canon*, Grand Rapids: Zondervan, 1986, 32.

10. Kevin J. Vanhoozer, 'The Semantics of Biblical Literature: Truth and Scripture's Diverse Literary Forms', in *ibid.*, 53-104, notes 374-383.

11. Roger Lundin, Anthony C. Thiselton, & Clarence Walhout, *The Responsibility of Hermeneutics*, Grand Rapids: Eerdmans & Exeter: Paternoster, 1985, 129 pp.

had a reality of their own'.[12] But this was lost. A 'great reversal' took place: interpretation became a matter of fitting the biblical story into another world with another story rather than incorporating that world into the biblical story'.[13] The *locus* of meaning changed: no longer in the text, as it is, it merged, on the one hand, with the writer's intention, soon to be understood in terms of the cultural setting (the first main area of study); on the other hand, the meaning was identified with the reference, either the ostensive reference of historical fact, under Locke's influence in England, or the ideal reference of the truth taught by the text, in the wake of Chr. Wolff's analysis in Germany. Obviously, philosophy played an important part; even before such thinkers as Locke and Wolff, the dominance of the subject-object scheme, the basic structure of humanism, was decisive. The pressures of apologetic urgencies also contributed to the eclipse of the text itself.

The implication, which Frei would not suppress, is that we should go back to the text as it is, to the Bible as it presents itself. The 'fundamental presupposition', Mark Ellingsen spells out, is that it presents itself 'as literature'.[14] Historical critics and their orthodox opponents both ignored the obvious nature of the books of Scripture: works of art, 'poems' or 'a poem' of many parts, using the word poem in a way which tries to revive its etymological sense (*poiéma*). Such is the emphasis on artistic quality that some decorate the new proposals with the name 'aesthetic theology'.[15]

Yet we must still highlight 'narrative'. Among the various literary forms woven into Scripture, narrative prose stands supreme. It enjoys pride of place, quantitatively and qualitatively. Other literary genres have a subordinate role, *e.g.* the Epistles, and are grafted upon the main story.[16] The whole Bible, beginning with Genesis and ending with Revelation, as one grand narrative; N. Frye remarks that it is U-shaped, after the pattern of comedy – the Bible as a whole

12. Frei, 90.
13. *Ibid.*,130.
14. Ellingsen, 88.
15. Vanhoozer, 374 n.5, announces a forthcoming article under that title.
16. Ellingsen, 90f.

is a truly divine comedy.[17] Biblical narrative is of the *realistic* kind, in most instances. Hans Frei recalls Erich Auerbach's judgement: there have been three high points in the realistic tradition: the Bible, Dante's *Divina Commedia,* and the realistic novel of modern times, especially in XIXth century France, the roots in XVIIIth century England.[18]

Aesthetic narrative theology is breaking new ground. Orthodox commentators in the past have shown appreciation for the beauty and integrity of the stories of Scripture, but they had no methodology to go further; instead, they spent (or wasted?) their energy in efforts to demonstrate accurate correspondence with external facts. Those of the *heilsgeschichtliche Schule* did celebrate the patterns of Biblical narrative, but they were interested in the kerygma, in the confession of the 'God Who Acts', not in the art of story telling.

In contrast, narrative theologians extol the form itself of the story. To think that one could replace it by a set of abstract propositions is to fall into pitiful illusion. It is not just a matter of dullness as opposed to colour and pleasure. If one renounces the story-form, one loses the force, the real effect, the actual meaning of what is told. Stories are so popular because they address the whole man, and deeper human levels than ratiocination. Man is revealed in that he tells stories and enjoys following them.

The main objective of Paul Ricoeur's masterly *Temps et récit* is to establish the reciprocal determination, the basic correlation, between time and narrative. To a large extent, he does succeed. Only narrative can bridge the gulf between phenomenological time (the line of Augustine, Husserl, Heidegger) and cosmological time (the line of Aristotle, and of Kant in his own way): we must conjoin them, and yet we cannot do so, except through narrative. Ricoeur goes even further: the answer to the question 'Who?', the question of the personal subject who lives from birth to death, can only be told as a story.'The story', he writes, 'tells the *who* of the action'. *The identity of the who, therefore, is nothing else*

17. Frye, *Le Grand Code*, 236.
18. Frei, 15.

than a narrative identity.'[19] This is valid not only for the *ipse* of individuals, but for communities as well, *e. g.* for Israel. [20]

The glory of narrative form eclipses, in its turn! preoccupation with such reality as may lie beyond, 'out there'. Whether or not particular occurrences in time and space correspond with the stories has little relevance indeed. Although moderate and cautious, Hans Frei sees the meaning of the gospel narrative and the problem of Jesus' messiahship in actual, historical, fact as 'different questions altogether'.[21] He warns that historical likelihood does not follow from history-likeness.[22] N. Frye, who, more freely, holds aloof from traditional Christianity, rejects subordination to non-verbal realities.[23] For Ellingsen, since the significance of Scripture is not bound to historical reference, historical criticism can no more undermine its meaningfulness than it could in the case of *MacBeth*.[24] We could compare with an older classic: had Heinrich Schliemann failed to unearth the remains of Troy, the *Iliad* would have lost nothing of its significance. Ellingsen cares to make an exception for Christ's resurrection; he concedes that a decisive historical proof *against* it would count as a refutation of the Christian faith.[25] But this is the exception, and not entirely free from ambiguity, for Ellingsen considers that the affirmation of the factual character of the resurrection is both unverifiable and meaningless. The burden of the new proposals hangs on the well-known motto: *the meaning of the poem is within the poem*!

Narrative champions find warm permission to play referential meaning down in the cultural climate of the times. Stucturalists, as we note, already, have shut language upon itself, and similarly excluded reference in their study of texts: their whole method depends on their decision to take longer units of discourse as analogous to Saussure's *langue* (not

19. Ricoeur, *Temps et récit*, III, 355.
20. *Ibid.*, 357.
21. Frei, 133.
22. *Ibid.*, 11f.
23. Frye, *Le Grand Code*, 75, 83ff, 129, 299f.
24. Ellingsen, 89.
25. *Ibid.*, 95.

parole), to an autonomous system of internal differences.[26] Other streams of influence converge with the formalist tendency: one remembers how Hans-Georg Gadamer's *Truth and Method* polemicizes against an instrumental view of language, and thus devalues its denotative function. From another philosophical horizon, the Wittgenstein's *Sprachspiele*, which are also forms of life, erase the earlier, most rigid (and short-sighted) referentialism of the *Tractatus*, although one of the games still consists in telling how things are.[27] The idea that literature and poetry, at least, are born when imagination cuts itself loose from the world of objective facts has become commonplace: most critics would concur that the status of art implies 'the *priority of lexis* over *logos*, such a use of language that ordinary reference is suspended or indeterminate.[28] This 'isolation and subsequent exaltation of the aesthetic category', this 'emphasis upon the self-contained, nonreferential, sacred nature of the work itself' belong already to the legacy of the late XVIIIth century, now come to full blossom.[29]

Some writers have gone so far as to attack the privilege of reference in historiography itself.[30] They were preceded, of course, by post-Kantian critiques of the idea of historical truth as correspondence; Raymond Aron had given to the anti-realist thesis the sharpness of his dialectics and the charm of his style, in his widely-acclaimed *Introduction `a la philosophie de l'histoire* (1938);[31] it is worth noting that, forty-five years later, he also was led to a *retractation* of the views he had defended as a young man.[32] Nevertheless, few have followed him along the path of this *metanoia*. One can hear from all around the indignant outcry 'Positivism!' if one

---

26. Ricoeur, 'Le mod`ele du texte: l'action sensée considérée comme un texte', in *Du texte `a l'action*, 206
27. As Vanhoozer, 83, timely reminds us.
28. Paul De Man as quoted by C. Walhout, 41 and, then, 40.
29. Well demonstrated by Lundin, 9.
30. Ricoeur deals with the views of Hayden White, *Temps et récit* I, 228ff; III, 220ff.
31. See again Ricoeur, *ibid.*, I, 139ff
32. Raymond Aron, *Mémoires. Cinquante ans de réflexion politique*, Paris; Julliard, 1983, 124.

dares ask of the past, in Ranke's words, *wie es eigentlich gewesen ist.* Narrative theologians (or thinkers, as they write of the Bible) show greater caution or restraint than many, on this matter – and, in practice, they do rely on the results of historical criticism in their handling of a number of texts – but whatever weakens the prestige of factual conformity strengthens their nonreferential inclination in Biblical studies.

What, then, is the *meaning* or *truth* of a narrative? The experience of meditating, imbibing, a poem, or living through a novel – it changes lives, [33] points us to the answer. Literature wields a strange power of presence: 'The Bible', says N. Frye, 'lays aside referential meaning; it is not a book which denotes a historical presence outside of itself, but a book which identifies itself with this presence. In the end, the reader too is invited to identify himself with the book'.[34] Generally, 'the poet's job is not to tell you what happened, but what happens',[35] to illuminate the baffling chaos of brute experience. Art brings order and light out of confusion. In like vein, Ricoeur writes of fiction and narratives: 'the plots that we invent help us to give configuration to our confused, amorphous, ultimately dumb, temporal experience';[36] they resemble scientific 'models' in heuristic function.[37] Often, he highlights the 'proposal of a world' into which we can 'project our most genuine possibilities' (a phrase borrowed from Heidegger).[38] He seems to mean both an interpretation of the world as it is and a scheme for a better world, a scheme to guide our hopes and endeavours through the toil and struggle of our days. Hans Frei also defines 'the peculiar way in which realistic narrative means or makes sense' as 'the endeavour to set forth a temporal world'.[39] For Ricoeur, self and world are correlatives, and the virtue of narrative is

---

33. As Ellingsen emphasizes, 93.
34. Frye, *Le Grand Code*, 200.
35. Frye, *The Educated Imagination*, as quoted by Leland Ryken, *Triumphs of the Imagination*, Downers Grove,Ill.: IVP, 1979, 94.
36. Ricoeur,*'De l'interprétation'*, in *Du texte à l'action*, 17.
37. Ricoeur, *L'imagination dans le discours et dans l'action*, in *ibid.*,221
38. Ricoeur, *'Herméneutique et critique des idéologies'*, in *ibid.*, 368f.
39. Frei, 150f.

similarly to mould the subject, to enlarge or enrich the self;[40] we already saw that narrative is the very foundation of selfhood.

With imperial power, Ricoeur insists that such truth and meaning are *not* nonreferential. Rather, the suspension of superficial, ordinary, ostensive, reference frees fiction for a deeper reference.[41] He will not abandon the old Aristotelian word, *mimésis*. He will not renounce what he calls the 'ontological vehemence' of language;[42] 'if one eliminates this referential function, there is left only an absurd game of erring signifiers',[43] the structural theory of myth would be reduced to 'a necrology of the meaningless discourses of mankind'.[44] Metaphors have an ontological power of 'redescription' of reality, and narratives, an ontological power of 'refiguration' of temporal experience, of human action; he gladly makes Nelson Goodman's formula his own: 'Reality Remade'.[45] However, one should not oppose too sharply Ricoeur's deeper ontological reference and the more provocative denial of reference by other narrativists: in both arguments literature is not interested in a concordance between statements and definite states of affairs in the real world; its significance derives from intra-textual relationships, and only radical quasi-nihilists would refuse some connections with our lives, whether explained in terms of ontological reference or not.[46]

Ricoeur enriches still his reflections on the value and truth of fiction in praising the beauty and benefits of *imagination*; it is the source of the precious 'iconic increase', also in stories

40. Ricoeur, *'De l'interprétation'*, 31 and *'Herméneutique et critique des idéologies'*, 368f
41. Ricoeur, *Temps et récit*, I, 119f, which recalls the Seventh Study, already, of *La Métaphore vive*, 1975,; in fact, in the later work, Ricoeur prefers to speak of refiguration than to use the language of reference, III, 230f. Wolfgang Iser, quoted by Walhout, 54, comes close to the idea of a price paid for significance; see Ricoeur, *ibid*.III, 248 n.2, for the exact distance he puts between Iser's nonreferentiality of literature and his own thesis.
42. *Ibid.*, I, 80, cf. 118; and *'De l'interprétation'*, 34, (and *passim*).
43. Ricoeur, *'Le mod`ele du texte...'*, 189
44. *Ibid.*, 208.
45. Ricouer, *Temps et récit*, 1, 122.
46. Walhout, 46, who criticizes also Ricoeur.

told.[47] Imagination is the necessary ally of possibility, play, freedom. Imagination frees us from the clutches of Necessity.[48]

A piece of literature, also, functions as a member of the whole corpus of existing texts. The systematic outworking of this insight has been the major original contribution of N. Frye.[49] Ricoeur, who sometimes evokes Gadamer's *Sprachlichkeit* (linguistically) in the same sense,[50] broadens the analysis of narrative efficiency to the dimension of culture; man has a *Welt*, not only an *Umwelt*, by virtue of all the texts he has read.[51] In an earlier work, Ricoeur pondered the link between the German word *Bildung*, education, and *Bild*, image.[52] In the Judaeo-Christian tradition, the dominant images, or figures, of the Exodus, the Resurrection, the Coming Kingdom, have the function of educating us, moulding world and self.[53]

An artistic story, yes

If we compare the aesthetic narrative approach to others which prevailed before, its appeal and rewards can hardly be denied. Rhetorical criticism has yielded admirable results, *e.g.* in the hands of Luis Alonso-Schökel and several of his fellow-Jesuits. We rejoice when it is introduced to the evangelical public.[54] According to Hans Frei, Dr Johnson outlawed

---

47. Ricoeur, *'L'imagination dans le discours et dans l'action'*, 213-236.
48. Already in 1964, Ricoeur, in *'La critique de la religion et le langage de la foi'*, *Bulletin du Centre Protestant d'Etudes*, Geneva, 16/4-5, June 1964, 31 complained against the hermeneutics of suspicion of Marx and Freud that they did not make room for 'the grace of imagination' (Spinozistic temptation).
49. See comments by Lundin, 14, and Todorov's introduction to *Le Grand Code*.
50. Ricoeur, *'Herméneutique et critique des idéologies'*, 351.
51. Ricoeur, *Temps et récit*, I, 121, *et passim*.
52. Ricoeur, *De l'interprétation Essai sur Freud*, Paris: Seuil, 1965, 503
53. Ricoeur, *'Herméneutique philosophique et herméneutique biblique'*, in Francois Bovon & Gregoire Rouiller, Ed., *Exegesis. Probl`emes de méthode et exercices de lecture*, Neuchatel & Paris: Delachaux & Niestlé, 1975, 226f
54. See Ryken's work quoted n.35, and his new *Words of Delight*, Baker, 1987.

brutally all application of literary considerations to Scripture;[55] we may say our *Nostra culpa* for having too often obeyed him, for having too often read the Bible as Philistines. . . .

We may call the Bible 'literature' in spite of the notorious difficulty in defining the word[56] and a 'work of art', a 'poem' if you will. From one point of view, at least, it may stand as a rightful description.

We should be wary, however, of misleading connotations creeping in. The Bible was not written primarily for the entertainment of its readers, whereas, according to N. Frye's *Anatomy of Criticism*, 'in literature, what entertains is prior to what instructs, or, as we may say, the reality-principle is subordinate to the pleasure-principle.[57] The Bible, Holy Scripture, functions as the Covenant treaty document, as Meredith. G. Kline so cogently argued; it is *canon*, the rule of faith and conduct. Nor is the *primacy of form* a likely feature of the Law and the Prophets. Only, the divinely inspired writers used the tools and resources of artistic expression; their writings exhibit wonderful craft and subtlety: in composition, in invention (especially the reworking of existing literary *genres*), in the clever weaving of themes, and exploitation of symbolic valencies. Subtlety! Consummate poets and writers they show themselves to be, as they discreetly hide the devices they put to use. The eulogy of Qoheleth, at the end of his book, recalls the excellency his art attained. If we avoid reduction, if we pay due attention to differences, we may acknowledge that Scripture, for the quality of its form, does rank among the masterpieces of literature (they would be few who would gainsay this judgment!).

To a large extent, we may also concur with the privilege recognized to *narrative*. As regards mere space allotted, the preponderance of the story form may not be so overwhelming as narrative theologians suggest; Wisdom literature, the Prophetical books (*posteriores*) and the Psalms, didactic material in the New Testament, finally constitute a huge mass of texts. However, they are taken up into a main Narrative, as

55. Frei, 103.
56. Vanhoozer, 378 n. 101.
57. As quoted by Lundin, 14.

Dooyeweerd well perceived when he identified the ground-motive of the Biblical Revelation as the threefold scheme *Creation-Fall-Redemption*. It does espouse the shape of a U, although – and this might prove significant for our concern – it is non-symmetrical U, the second branch being higher than the first one: the New Man, who comes from above, a life-giving spirit, provides more than edenic restoration; paradise regained with Christ outmatches even the perfect paradise we lost. As to the art of story-telling in the Bible, it has been for the enchantment of generations, whether Samson's feats are narrated, or Elijah's combats and miracles, or Paul's adventurous journeys. We may admire the account of our Lord's passion in the Gospels as a narrative model – if we dare, when treading such holy ground, consider style and composition.

The meaningfulness of fiction, the truth-value it holds, need not be denied. A flexible and diversified notion of truth can be at home within an evangelical theology,[58] and it is rash and wrong to confuse fiction and falsehood, generally, in front of history and truth.[59] Fiction *per se* may bring us the Word of God, we readily grant it. Imagination belongs to the excellent creation gifts from above; it does signal man's created transcendence, his ability to step back, to free himself from immediate involvement in empirical reality, and thus, to pass judgements over it, to draw interpretations of it, to design transformations as well.

Part of the effect of Bible reading in the Church, among believers, did obtain after the manner of fictional efficacy – as described by Hans Frei, N. Frye, Paul Ricoeur. Many, while captivated by the stories, have had little concern for historical references. For centuries, the grand Biblical Narrative *de facto* informed European culture in the way of myth; the sacred story provided essentially *Bildung*. This much we feel constrained to concede.

However, common belief remained that the things told had taken place. As with myth where myth is alive, it is a serious question whether the story can fulfil its role without the 'naive' credence that it did happen though *illo tempore*. Above

58. It is the thrust of Vanhoozer's essay.
59. Walhout, 75ff.

all, is the attitude of comparative disinterest for events, as objective occurrences in ordinary time, *true to the Bible itself?* The practice of centuries may represent a deviation, calling for reformation! It will be our argument that the narrative approach, as exemplified by writers whom we have named, deals with one aspect only of the Biblical phenomenon and misses *what constitutes itss original force*; a rehabilitation of referential meaning appears to be both feasible and timely.

Yet history first

It is high time, indeed, that one should challenge the prevalent nonreferential emphases. The mission is easiest in the case of *historiography*, since Ricoeur himself has shown how impossible it is to efface the historian's interest in what happened, the control which documentary evidence exercises over reconstruction, his intention to repay a debt to the past, or Ricoeur says, to the dead; 'in contrast with the novel, the historian's constructions intend to be reconstructions of the past. Through documentary evidence, the historian submits *to what, once, was*'.[60] Even borrowing schemes from fiction does not obliterate this trait.[61] Since Ricoeur's efforts aim at establishing the solidarity which binds together the two forms of narrative, historical and fictional, his is a weighty witness: in sober lucidity, he had to register the difference. One could strike even more strongly, and lay stress on *witness* (instead of 'trace', as Ricoeur chooses[62]), and on a debt which we owe not only to the dead, but to God. Clarence Walhout offers remarkable insights on the issue; without forgetting to list criteria for discriminating history from fiction, he brings into sharp focus the distinctive claim of historical writing:

> In a historical text ... we encounter not only the author's interpretation of the events but also the claim that the events being interpreted were actual events. The author's statements count as interpretive assertions about actual events.[63]

60. Ricoeur, *Temps et récit*, III, 204.
61. *Ibid.*, 271.
62. *Ibid.*, 175ff, 266f.
63. Walhout, 75.

The key-concept he introduces is that of *authorial stance*; the authorial stance differs in the two great types of narrative, and Walhout convincingly shows that it cannot be reduced, even on the formal plane, to the formalists' narrative voice or implied author.[64] (A significant correlation: nonreferential orientations tend to eliminate both author and referent: the hypostasis of the text devours both subject and object, reality before and reality beyond.) Ricoeur's cautious rebuttal of the absorption of history by story and Walhout's firm and fine analysis are enough to warn us against under-estimates of factual reference.

As to *language* as such, Ricoeur again has valiantly resisted nonreferential views, and we have alluded to his protest; although he blunts the edge of his own refutation of structuralism when he separates ordinary, empirical (ontic?) referentiality and the deeper ontological vehemence of poetical, 'festive', language.[65] Robust opposition comes again from the speech-act theory quarter. Austin and Searle have discerned that all illocutionary acts, not only assertions, have to do, in more or less complicated ways, with states of affairs.[66] Walhout strongly pleads that 'the meanings are not lodged in the words *per se* but in our continued use of words for certain purposes . . .'[67] nonreferential language is such a nonsense, a square circle, that he maintains 'in the case of fiction the language refers descriptively to fictional states of affairs', while he uses *mimesis* for the relationship to the real world.[68] Coming from another tradition, the Roman Catholic exegete and theologian Rene Laurentin stresses: 'Through his usual linguistic and conceptual schemes, man aims at reality and reaches to reality'.[69] And again: 'What is important is that

---

64. *Ibid.*, 69ff; 48f, 64, 66.
65. The theme of the 'language *en fête*' appears already in *'La structure, le mot, l'événement'* of 1967, republished in Ricoeur's *Le Conflit des interprétations*, Paris: Seuil, 1969, 95; the theme of the third, deeper, level, of the 'dire' is a common theme is his hermeneutical writings.
66. Vanhoozer, 87, 91, 95, 97.
67. Walhout, 46.
68. *Ibid.*, 52, 55f.
69. René Laurentin, *'Vérité des Evangiles de l'Enfance'*, Nouvelle Revue Théologique, 105, 1983, 695.

the knowing subject should so decipher the elements transmitted to him that he arrives at the object: art the other quâ other, in symbolic fashion, to be sure, but authentically'.[70] The present reversal of the direction of the flow, he suggests, might have something to do with the spread of homosexuality.[71] In Scripture, the giving of names, already in the first two chapters of Genesis, as a key operation in the relationship of a person to another person or to a lower creature, points to a referential view; so does the distinction between word and fulfilment in prophetic discourse.

Does artistic language necessarily, or normally, suspend reference to the real world, or states of affairs within it? This is far from certain. Even poems in the narrower sense of the term do not always keep their meaning in themselves, or in a projected world of pure imagination. When Ronsard writes a sonnet to persuade a young lady that she should yield to his advances, much of the meaning in the poem seems to refer to external reality. 'In frequent instances,' Walhout notes, 'the referents of fictional texts are to be found in the actual world as well as in the fictional world'.[72] Gnomic and didactic poetry, the epic celebration of a king's campaigns, all look beyond the delight radiating from their form. Narratives, especially of the realistic kind, not seldom maintain a referential aim: history as told by Gibbon or Michelet involves the full range of an artist's resources, it is a well-wrought story, a work of art; yet, factual reference may hardly pass for an indifferent matter. Vanhoozer is able to quote from a literary critic, Gerald Graff, who dissents from the majority view, from the Romanticist dualism of poetic and ordinary discourses,[73] and from another, Susan S. Lanser, who 'is concerned to rebuke modern literary critics who deny the referential nature of literature: "Literature: is communicative both in usage and intent, and the distinction between 'literary'

70. *Ibid.*, 698.
71. *Ibid.*, 699
72. Walhout, 122n.51; he gives as examples London and Paris in Dickens' *A Tale of Two Cities*, Nat Turner in William Styron's *The Confessions of Nat Turner*.
73. Vanhoozer, 70, 72f.

and 'ordinary' language which poeticians have tended to assume is not supported by linguistic research'."[74] Nothing warrants the mutual exclusion of ostensive, real, reference, and deeper, ontological significance: the same text can both tell accurately how things, particular things, are in actual fact, and build a model for the understanding of life, and this in rapturous words.[75]

Some artistic narrative, indeed, the bulk of modern artistic narrative, is fictional and devoid of precise historical reference. Does this apply with fair probability to the *Biblical* story and stories? The foregoing observations can prove that it would be rash to affirm it *a priori,* as a necessary concomitant of aesthetic excellence; but, upon inspection, it might still be the case. Narrative theology would enjoy a large measure of justification, even with a referential doctrine such as Walhout's, if the Bible functioned in ways similar to that of XIXth century realistic novels. How does the situation appear?

There are stories exempt of ostensive, particular, reference in Scripture, and the example of parables comes to mind. Textual and contextual indicators leave no doubt, though many parables have a direct historical reference: Nathan's story told to David – Thou art the man! – or the parable of the wicked husbandmen and the Son put to death, or of the sower going out to scatter seed. . . . There are a few stories for which the import of the indicators we have is subject to debate: we would take the parable of Lazarus and the rich man as fictional, we would defend the historical nature of Esther and Jonah, but some evangelicals would care to differ. As to the great number of history-like narratives in Scripture, however, we are not aware of any hints that we should read them as non-historical. Artistic concerns are definitely subordinate to other intentions, even in Wisdom writings. Complex compositions, intricate adornment, elaborate symmetries, may point away from an overly literal or crude interpretation (*e.g.* in Genesis 1), but they are not likely to suppress generally the basic reference to space-time events 'out there'.

74. *Ibid.*, 91
75. A. C. Thiselton, *The Responsibility of Hermeneutics*, 100.

More than once, the authors voice a clear, or acute, preoccupation of historical correspondence. The Second Epistle of Peter rejects emphatically any assimilation of the gospel story with 'cleverly devised tales' – artfully framed fictional narratives – and stresses the testimony of eye-witnesses (1:16). Luke's prologue explains and defines the writer's intention, his authorial stance, and grounds the certainty, infallibility *(a-sphaleia)*, of the message upon its concordance with the facts. Many years ago, Jacques Ellul had recognized in this passage a perfect statement of the Christian historian's method and point of view.[76] The Fourth Gospel insists heavily on the reliability of the Disciple's testimony: he saw and testified (1935) – and throughout Scripture, the enormous importance of the category of witness witnesses indeed against the fictional hypothesis. . . .

There is a sneaking suspicion that such a hypothesis would have occurred to none, had not historical criticism as currently practised, destroyed confidence in the witness of Biblical texts. Narrative theology sometimes looks like a strategy for maintaining the value and profitability of the text, in spite of doubts as to their basis in reality; or, we may say, for salvaging a Word of God in the Bible, whether or not its assertions are true to fact.[77]

The question, then, rebounds: does not the Biblical conviction that the things told did so happen simply reflect the candid naivety of a pre-critical age? Are we not in a position enabling us better to discern the true value and meaning of the Bible than the Biblical writers themselves? In many cases, the Bible deluded itself in thinking to be history what we know is story, fictional story!

Imputation of naivety is a risky move; it may always boomerang on you. Of the two, the wise master in ancient time and the modern scholar armoured with critical methodology, the more naive may not be the one we expect. The naivety of believing one has outgrown naivety. . . . We cannot attempt to meet here the arguments of those who deny

---

76. Jaques Ellul, *'Note problématique sur l'histoire de l'Eglise', Foi et Vie*, 47, 1949, 314ff.
77. Ellingsen's intention is clearly to reconcile evangelicals and current criticism .

the historical trustworthiness or exactness of Biblical information; we depend on the work of others, who fulfil this learned task with growing recognition, as they walk in the footsteps of such knights of erudite faith, in generations past, as were Sir William Ramsay and William Henry Green. We may only mention the progress of criticism, in sensitive areas, which uncovers features in Biblical narratives and fiction coherent with historical claims. The Jewish scholar, Stuart Lasine, has underlined the formal differences and elsewhere, especially at the level of indicators.[78] Even the story of Eden should not be too hastily classified as 'myth', warns Pierre Gibert, of the Facultes Catholiqués of Lyons; 'however paradoxical it may sound, in the story of Adam and Eve the three components of historical narrative are to be found', namely, the continuity with ordinary time, the action of responsible, complex characters, and an implied, again complex, evaluation.[79] There is a consistency which embraces the conviction of the Biblical writers that they spoke of actual events, whether naively or not, and the way they wrote.

The knot of the matter from a more theological angle (the dogmatician's) is the *essential* part which historical reference plays in Biblical religion. Because it is the very soul of Biblical faith, it cannot be laid aside as a secondary concern while the *Bildung* or imagination - shaping function slides to the centre. With most myths and folklore stories, popular belief in the reality of events may be shaken – what is essential in them remains still. In spite of a probable loss in efficacy, one can argue that the deeper intention of myth being to neutralize historical succession and its fear (both Mircea Eliade and Claude Levi-Strauss here agree), and mythical time being 'no-time' in disguise, the force of myth can be divorced from historical reference. Not so with the Bible: remove the facticity of its referents, it is emptied of its meaning, faith becomes worthless, we are the most miserable among all men. It is an either/or, an all-or-nothing debate: either true

---

78. Stuart Lasine,'Fiction, Falsehood and Reality in Hebrew Scripture', *Hebrew Studies* 25, 1984, 24-40, as quoted and praised by an alumni letter of Elmer B. Smick, February 1986.
79. Pierre Gibert, *Bible, Mythes et récits de commencement*, Paris: Seuil, 1986, 100, cf. 91, 97, 115.

history, or the most perverse of all illusions; there is no intermediate category, under the label 'story', which can salvage one half and let the other half go.[80]

Is our radical antithesis a *true* simplification, one apt to reveal the truth of the debate? Or is it a simplistic distortion, the result of yielding to an extremist temptation? To warrant our making the contrast, the appeal goes to the massive phenomenological difference between the Judaeo-Christian message and myths or religious doctrines on every hand: Mircea Eliade, above all others, brought it to the fore. The radical break from mythical thought, he saw, happened in the Old Testament, with a personal God intervening in history, revealing himself within time;[81] this conception, 'revived and amplified by Christianity', makes its most original feature,[82] the centrality of the once for all saving Event, in the very time of life.[83] Eliade does not pursue much further on this route he so clearly traces, for he observes that the mythical (no)-time of cyclic repetition, acted out in ritual, has invaded back the Church - but *after* the New Testament.[84] If we keep to the *Sola Scriptura*, the sheer uniqueness of the Christian reference to a completed redemption, accomplished at a particular place in our days, 'under Pontius Pilate', make it unlikely that one could de-historicize the Gospel as one can the Oedipus myth. It is Gospel, News!

The Apostle binds together the singular event of the cross and the singular event of the fall (Romans. 5:12ff). Just as the Gospel is unique among discourses of salvation, the Biblical

---

80. For a fuller treatment and other quotations, we may mention our previous work in *'Le mythe et l'Evangile'*, Revue Réformée 19/75-76, 1968, 56-65; *'L'Evangile, mythe ou histoire'*, in Henri Blocher & F. Lovsky, *Bible & Histoire*, Lausanne: Presses Bibliques Universitaires, 1980, 29-57; and the seventh chapter in our *In the Beginning. The Opening Chapters of Genesis*, transl. by David G. Preston, Leicester: IVP, 1984, with a discussion of Ricoeur's insights and arguments.

81. Mercea Eliade, *Le Mythe de l'Eternel Retour*, Idées; Paris: Gallimard, 1969, 124f.

82. *Ibid.*, 124.

83. *Ibid.*, 166.

84. *Ibid.*, 165; also from Eliade, *Aspects du mythe*, Idees; Paris; Gallimard, 1963, 205ff.

story of the beginnings of man is unique in assigning an origin not metaphysical, but historical, to evil. Better than anybody else, Ricoeur has drawn the contrast and expressed its significance:

> Creation is good from the first; it proceeds from a Word and not from a Drama; it is complete. Evil, then, can no longer be identical with a prior and resurgent chaos; a different myth will be needed to account for its appearance, its 'entrance into the world'. History, too, then, is an original dimension and not a 're-enactment ' of the drama of creation. It is History, not Creation, that is a Drama. Thus Evil and History are contemporaneous. . . . . Evil becomes scandalous at the same time as it becomes historical.[85]

He has seen the consonance with ethical monotheism, with the prophetic indictment and psalmic confession of sin, as well as with the historical character of salvation. Although he tragically falls back on the common mythical assessment of Genesis 2 and 3, and so disfigures partially the meaning he has discerned, the fruit of his lucidity remains. It convinces us that the specific doctrine of evil taught by Scripture (not metaphysical) depends on the truth of historical reference in the passages concerned. Thereby, we can gain a theological understanding of the essential role it plays in the Christian message.

Other original features of Biblical religion stem from the same solidarity. Redemption *ephapax* excludes the great mythical function of ritual, which, reiterated, makes the archetypal Events (or non-Events) present and effective. Redemption completed – *tetelestai* – excludes also the usual perspective of works to be done by men that they may reach out to deity. God did it; it already happened; therefore, salvation is not of works – not even of works of art!

Narrative theology focuses on Scripture as a *work*, and as such, relatively self-contained. But first and foremost, it should be received as the *Word*. As the Word, it refers to reality, it says something definite on the real state of mankind, and on the real victory won over real sin and death; it leads faith not to enlightening symbols first, but to the saving Event

---

85. Ricoeur, trans. by Emerson Buchanan, 1967, *The Symbolism of Evil*, Boston : Beacon, 1967,, 203.

in its real density. As the Word, it leads transparently to the Event without adding to the Event.

As the Word, Scripture reveals the *Person* speaking. Is it a mere matter of subjective taste? In much narrative theology, we feel a strange absence of God. The human artist's work is praised; it is credited with the proposal of a *world* – in fact, partial sketches of more or less modified segments of the world.[86] But the *God* of the word remains as if unknown. A pantheistic undercurrent tries to fill the vacuum in N. Frye's convergent interpretation of the Bible, of oriental religions, and gnosticism in between.[87] The Bible is *the Word of God*, leading to him who spoke, and speaks, through the Prophets and through the Son! One disobeys Scripture if one stops at Scripture, this instrument. One obeys Scripture if one reads in order to reach beyond, to the Event, to the Author.

In the light of the manifold contrast, our conclusion might be a warning: the danger that threatens aesthetic narrative emphases is that of an idolatrous trust in narrative as such, whereas there is salvation only in him, and his historical work, to whom the Biblical narrative refers. The beauty which narrativists rightfully praise may become, as in all idols, a snare. Lonely man, estranged from nature, destined surely to die, man bearing unbearable guilt, naturally hopes in language, the subject-object medium, that it will humanize the world and become a home for him. He naturally looks to the best his art can produce for comfort, for the soothing integration of evil, of death, in the order of being: 'Through mythology, man dodges aesthetically evil', as he vainly tries, in Plotinus ' words 'to capture evil in the bonds of beauty'.[88] He naturally resorts to narrative, through whose '*concordia discors*' he may dream of taming time, the frightening flow. But only the real God of the Word, who acted in history, can deliver us from cosmic loneliness, and guilt, and death. The artistic story which tells us so is *history first* : we are saved.

---

86. Wallhout, quoting from Nicholas Wolterstorff, judiciously recalls the partial character of the projected ' worlds' of literature, 66.
87. Frye, *Le Grand Code*, 161f, 183, 234.
88. Etienne Borne, *Le Problème du mal*, Paris: Presses Universitaires de France, 1967[4], 51.